Deer in the Headlamps

Out of Work at Fifty Years of Age

by
Ray Austin Kampa

PublishAmerica

Baltimore

First printing

ISBN: 1-4137-0667-3
PUBLISHED BY PUBLISHAMERICA, LLLP
www.publishamerica.com
Baltimore

Printed in the United States of America

For all who have passed this way—
or will someday

Introduction

I've written this personal record of my experiences with unemployment to inform, to entertain, and to register my complaints about a system that doesn't seem to be working. If you are currently unemployed and seeking work, perhaps you'll recognize some of your emotions reflected within these pages, and if so, I encourage you to read out loud, at the top of your lungs, perhaps on the steps of your state capital, those passages that hit home. Lord knows I've ranted plenty around our house—with varying results. It is best, though, to rail at the powers and not your loved ones.

Throughout the chapters, I've added stories about deer camp, traveling by motorcycle, things that have happened throughout my career, and even brief explanations of technical and political situations. The time frame tends to move forward like a journal, but it also bounces around now and then to remind the reader of context and to expound in different contexts. The intended effect is to put a sense of forward movement, backsliding, stagnating, and moving ahead once again—just like the way things go with extended periods of unemployment.

Some psychologists have compared the experience of unemployment with the breakup of a close relationship or a death in the family. Yes, that fits, but the emotions can be even more complex and difficult to handle because basic survival is also a looming issue. I've tried to express just how hard and dangerous all this is as the news announces ever more job losses in our country. We hear the numbers, but do we have a sense for what this really means for people? If you are there, you know what this means. If not, you may be fearing the future: What happens after the layoff? How bad can things get? What can you do to keep body, mind, and spirit together—and relationships?

I don't claim to have all the answers—nobody can claim that. We all go through our crisis periods differently, under varying circumstances, and with diverse levels of support from former employers, families, friends, and possibly governments. But I do have some answers, some suggestions, and some insights into what can often feel like cruel torture, and what can also be used to find both inner strength and latent talents.

Those who know me will recognize just what an emotional mess I can often be: sometimes a rough, cursing motorcycle maniac blasting blues harmonica, sometimes the reflective intellectual, sometimes the nice guy who cries over sad or happy movies. Yes, I confess: There is a multiplicity of personality in me, and I'm the first to say that I'm no treat to live with—you can ask Lydia, my significant other, about that. She laughs about flirtatious women, saying that they have no idea how hard it is to break in a guy like me. But one thing she knows she can count on, and that is no matter what kinds of upheavals are going on inside, I am always honest about them.

And so, this book. A collection of stories, observations, rants, suggestions, and a whole lot of honesty about long-term unemployment. I hope it helps.

~ *1* ~
A Story I Once Heard

Johnny crouched over in his straight-backed kitchen chair, and placing his hands palms outward alongside his grizzled head, he imitated the ear movements of the whitetail deer he was describing as the rest of us looked on. My father sat at the kitchen table across from Johnny. Rick, my oldest brother, lounged in an old, overstuffed chair, his legs thrown over one side. Rolph, my next older brother, sat backwards in a chair with his thickly muscled arms propped up by the chair back, his square chin resting on his arms. The inside of Johnny's lake cabin felt warm and moist from a fire crackling away in a cast iron stove, a pot of water steaming on top. We were all dressed in traditional deer camp clothes: red woolen pants, flannel shirts and thick gray socks.

"He heard my boot crunch on that ice crust," Johnny whispered, "and I thought he'd be spooked off." Johnny's hands rotated this way and that as he peered at the wall. I could almost see imaginary antlers branching up from his temples. "But something else caught his attention. It was the headlamps of old Number 27, coming along the tracks. Those headlamps were bright then; the sun had gone down an hour before. The old buck stood there like stone, staring into the oncoming light."

We all laughed as Johnny let his jaw hang limp and his eyes glaze over. He was the best storyteller in deer camp. My father, Bob, wiped a tear from his eye with a thick, knarry working man's paw. Rick, the camp's talented deer slayer, chuckled brightly but reserved. Rolph rocked forward and back in his chair.

"Well, it was old Sandy Makinnen in 27's cab, and he isn't known for stopping for nothing as insignificant as some foolish buck caught up in his headlamps, so on came the headlamps, thirty, maybe forty mile an hour."

"I let out a holler: 'Get going, yah stupid buck!', but old Buck just stood there, frozen. No flag up, no ears moving, I knew he was gonna be a gonner before long—so I raised my ought-six, jacked in a cartridge (making as much commotion with the bolt as I could), and took a bead right on old Buck's left antler. Bang!" We all jumped.

Johnny let out a belly laugh. "That sure got old Buck to moving, you betcha. The impact of the slug took off one antler, and he jumped way up, out of reflex don't you know, straight off the tracks. He fell—whump! Down in the snow bank. Out cold."

"Sandy waved at me as he passed on his way back to pick up more iron ore from the Sliver pit. Being polite, I waved back. The racket of that old steam engine drowned out the sound of my shot for Sandy, but Gabby Pearson heard it. You remember old Gabby, dontcha? Game warden? Yeah, that one. Well, he comes trundling up from the side road where he'd been watching this whole thing all along."

"'Johnny,' he says, 'looks like you just took a deer after sunset!'" Gabby was standing next to the knocked out deer, his fists like this on his hips." Johnny stood up, pushed out his beer belly, and posed like a pompous *sumanabeech*, as Johnny was like to say. "'You know that's against the law,' says Gabby, 'I'm going to have to take you in, Johnny'"

Johnny sat down, raised his hands in the air and let them flop down to his knees. He gave us a look of utter disgust, dropped his head and shook it slowly back and forth as if he were contemplating all of humanity's foolishness throughout the ages. Raising his head back up slowly, he said with a shrug, "'Well, Gabby', I told him while making my way over there, 'I suppose we'd better dress out that buck. No use wasting good meat!'"

"So Gabby borrows my knife and proceeds to start by sawing away at old Buck's nuts. Right about then, old Buck decides it's time to wake up!" Johnny grabbed a wooden spoon from the kitchen table and knocked it between the back braces on an empty chair. "That's what it sounded like, old Buck's hooves against Gabby's head!"

"Old Gabby, he nearly got knocked cold himself. But he grabbed onto that crazy buck's neck and hollered, 'Shoot him, shoot him gawdammit all tah hell!' I hollered back, I can't shoot him! It's after sunset!"

Johnny waited for our wild laughter to die down. "Well, old Gabby had to let me go that time. Old Buck just lost himself part of his rack, but he got out of those headlamps coming down on him. He ran off once Gabby let go. Gabby was shook up and cut here and there from those wicked hooves, but he lived through that one." Then Johnny looked around the room, catching each of us with his mirthful eyes. "So let this be a lesson to you: Never try to cut the nuts off a knocked-out buck! Make sure he's a dead buck! That is, unless some game warden's about to take you in. Then lend him your knife—the dull one."

Johnny made us laugh so hard it hurt and our eyes watered. Those were good days, back in deer camp, during the 1960s, up in the almost pristine country of Northern Minnesota. Vietnam hadn't blasted the country apart yet, but the assassinations (Kennedy, King, Kennedy again) had happened. Everyone knew something was going on, just not what. The Beatles played on Ed Sullivan's show, but we were still wearing flattop hair cuts. To us, Elvis would always be the King of Rock, deer hunting would always be an honorable sport, and people would always smoke pretty much anywhere they wanted.

The course of life had settled into getting through high school, maybe doing some military service, come back and work in the mines, get married, have children, buy a house, work on a lake place, retire, fish, and then die—probably from boredom. But this kind of stability could only last for maybe one or two generations, and we were about to learn this.

Rick had turned nineteen and was trying to figure a way out of the draft. First he tried college—that didn't work, he wasn't the scholarly type—then marriage, and that didn't work either for getting out of the draft. He wound up joining the US Air Force to avoid being conscripted as expendable meat.

The recruiter made exaggerations about how certain Rick's future would be in the Air Force: one tour of duty and electronics training. The way this worked out was somewhat different. Rick did two tours of duty, one in Turkey and one in Vietnam, and his training shifted from electronics to load master—balancing the weight of whatever the plane was carrying. Some of that cargo consisted of dead Americans in body bags.

Rick got out of the Air Force in 1969 and came home to find his bags outside the door—his wife wanted a divorce, and he let her have it. The divorce, that is.

Rolph joined the National Guard when he turned nineteen in 1966. For a time when Vietnam was getting very hot, we worried that he would get called up for a tour of duty. This never materialized, and so Rolph married, had kids, bought a house, and followed the proscribed path of living in Northern Minnesota.

My number came up in 1971, and it was a lucky number:

261, unlikely to get drafted. President Johnson had tried to make the draft a little more fun by drawing lottery numbers by birth date. The lower the number, the more likely you were to be seeking some way out. But just to make certain, I went to college to get the student deferment. Well, that wasn't the whole reason I went to college. Rick advised me to try this route because, as he said, the women are of higher quality in college. Now there's something that can be argued, but that wasn't my primary reason for going either. I wanted to prove that I could make good grades.

When you grow up in a place like Northern Minnesota, you tend to take one of two directions in life: Either you love the dickens out of the place and want to stay forever, or you hate the place to pieces and can't wait to get the hell out. In high school, I wanted to get the hell out but decided that a job in the iron mines was probably my fate. People in my family did not go off to college and earn layered degrees to become professionals of some sort. No, we worked for others, collected our paychecks, pissed and moaned about management, took our weekends and vacations, and that was that.

I was only a C-average student throughout grammar and high school. Getting good grades wasn't important. Oh, maybe my mother would have liked an honor roll student in the family, and maybe I had the highest potential to do that, but for what purpose? If what my fate involved was to work semi-skilled labor for some company in an open pit iron ore mine, who cares about higher education? It all paid the same.

So, I focused on the things that were important in life: motorcycles, cars, and girls. I pulled straight A's in automotive shop. I taught myself motorcycle mechanics. I dated and went steady and practiced my night moves.

But all through my grammar and high school years, the

aptitude tests they gave us every so often kept showing a potential that I was not achieving. I was always grades ahead of the class in language skills. My mathematics skills weren't strong, but they were not average either. So why wasn't I pulling As and Bs? Why wasn't I on the honor roll?

Lack of study was the only reason. Why study to get good grades when you can just listen to the teachers, read the text once, and take the tests? Getting average grades would get me through to what really mattered: working a good-paying job in the mines, getting married, romping around with sex, having kids, and playing with motorcycles and cars. But something kept nagging at me about all these mundane, superficial, and rather drab plans. Something was causing me to hate my hometown and my predestined fate.

When high school graduation came in 1970, I felt depressed. Well, that was that. I had some good times, bad times, and a lot of humdrum, mind-numbing times. Among my elective classes, I took journalism and typing with some vague notion of writing for a hobby. I wanted to write adventure novels like Edgar Rice Burroughs, who is most famous for creating the Tarzan character. Other electives included chemistry and physics where I learned to use a slide rule. I really liked the slide rule. It made perfect sense to me and took a lot of the drudgery out of mathematics. I found some of the physics to be not very exciting, like calculating the trajectory of a cannonball. Yeah, I thought, I'll really need to know how to do that while working in an iron ore mine! Maybe if a dynamite blast hurls some big rock my way? Maybe then I could whip out my trusty slide rule and figure out which way to run? Naw. Maybe if I just run away from where the rock is about to land, using my common sense and natural survival instincts, that would suffice. And so, my grade for physics class suffered because I just didn't care about cannonballs.

While others of my classmates were off to wild parties in the woods on graduation night—sowing the seeds of future shotgun weddings and amazingly large premature birth babies—I spent a fairly lame, quiet evening at home. Now, my fate was sealed. The only thing that could bust me out of it, so I thought, was to get drafted or join up and go to Vietnam. Die at age nineteen or twenty. There, no more messing around with fate and no more feelings that I needed to get the hell out somehow. Meanwhile, I needed a job in the mines.

The mining companies would not hire me. Each one had a different story about my weak back—and this surprised me because I could lift a stripped big-block, eight-cylinder Chrysler engine without much problem. I couldn't do this straight from the ground, but I did slide such an engine block off a bench, braced it against my thighs, and skittered it over to another bench. I don't recommend that anyone try this without professional psychiatric help.

One company told me I had an extra vertebra. Another showed me on the x-ray where a lower back vertebra had a thin spot. Yet another came up with fused together lower back vertebrae.

I thought they were all bullshitting me. I also wondered why only one mining company doctor wanted to check out my colon—and he seemed to enjoy that part way too much. An eighteen-year-old virgin ought to be given a little explanation and warning before doing something like that. And I should have been given a freaking job offer for the trouble! I was quickly learning that the real world after high school serves up unexpected violations. An attitude was starting to form as I felt my options shrinking down to minimum wage labor for the rest of my life.

After working in a heavy equipment parts department for about nine months, and after discovering that my chances to be drafted were minimal, and after taking a three-week motorcycle trip through Canada to British Columbia, down to California, and across the northern Rockies back to Minnesota, I decided to try college.

The cheapest thing to try first was a local community college. My first quarter, winter of 1971, was a resounding success—I pulled a 3.8 GPA (Grade Point Average) off of eighteen credits. I had proven myself capable of being an honor roll student—finally! My college career moved from the community college to a state college in Mankato, and there I worked at maintaining a high GPA through my last two years.

Nixon was running the country, and I watched him resign in a little bar outside Santa Fe, New Mexico during the late summer of 1974. My chopped Honda motorcycle with the eight-inch extended fork, king-queen seat, sissy bar, highway pegs, and custom pipes waited for me outside the bar, and getting back on it to complete my three-week vacation before returning to my last year of college never felt more free. Man, I was sure happy not to have Nixon's problems! Imagine resigning from being President of the United States. That must have hurt.

By the time the spring of 1975 rolled around, Vietnam was no longer an issue, I had run out of school money, and jobs were scarce. I was only a handful of credits short of graduation, but had no way of paying for the rest and keeping my head above water over the summer. I took a full-time job with fast food management. That sucked, so I moved from Mankato to Minneapolis and worked in a warehouse for three years. That didn't suck as badly as fast food, but I still felt I could do better, having almost a BA degree in English with a speech minor.

To make this story short, I broke into the emerging computer industry around 1979 and worked my way up over the ensuing decades. Although many recessions came and went, I managed to stay employed except for fairly brief, never more than two months long, periods of unemployment.

Johnny's story wasn't mine yet. Mine was the story that preceded his—I was the buck with a magnificent rack of personal accomplishments, making good money as a large computing systems administrator, living where I preferred to live in the Colorado Rockies, and having nothing but a bright future ahead. Things were about to change.

~ *2* ~

Singing My Unemployment Blues

It's been over a year now that I have not had a real job. My health insurance has expired. All my savings are gone, leaving nothing for retirement. If it wasn't for Lydia, I'd probably be homeless and living out of the Jeep that isn't paid off, avoiding the law and the repossession folks from the bank. I've retained a bankruptcy lawyer who advises that I not complete the filing until I get a job with health insurance or make enough off of freelance/contract work to afford health insurance.

Last June (2002) I turned fifty years of age. The Hayman wildfire in Colorado had started two days before, and it was getting big. A huge plume of smoke drifted around our place, gagging us even with the windows closed, smelling evil. The fire was so intense that it created rain clouds made up of moisture from dying trees. The forest wept on us. We worried about evacuation and losing the house to fire. Better this than losing it to foreclosure, we thought. At least the house is insured. With this and other worries like unemployment and bad circulation in my legs acting up (phlebitis and thrombosis, potentially deadly stuff), I did not have a very good birthday. On top of this, I had just entered an age group that doesn't get hired very much during hard times—or good times for that matter.

So here I sit before a laptop computer, typing out a description of what it is like to be out of work at fifty years of age, wondering if this machine will need to be sold to help make a house payment or buy food, wondering if I should try to sell something like the Jeep since it has another two years of payments to go—feeling depressed and panicked, frozen like a deer caught in the headlamps of an oncoming iron ore train. Christmas is only five days away. Ho, ho, ho, awe fudge.

Lydia still works for the University of Phoenix, but it cut her pay significantly for what they call *on-ground* classes, or classes held in traditional rooms with a physically present teacher. She has drummed up work for online classes, and I help her by writing online lectures and reviewing student papers for grammatical, spelling, style, and clarity mistakes.

We have decided not to press onward to find full-time work for me. The holidays are stressful enough; we will pick up the serious job hunt after the first of the year. In any case, we probably have enough money coming in to make it for a few more months. I am seriously considering taking some sort of work—driving a parts truck or something—just to bring in a little extra money. Before getting laid off, I made very good money and had full benefits. That situation seems so far away now, as if it never happened.

Feeling like a deer caught in the headlamps is the worst of these times. My mind clamps shut, creativity becomes impossible, and hopelessness works its way into my soul like a parasitic worm, sucking all the good juices away. I hate this feeling. A few days ago, I took the worm by its neck and threw it far away. I made some cold calls in an attempt to drum up a freelance writing contract. That helped tremendously, even though nobody wanted my services. One person did want to see my resume, and so I sent her one composed to emphasize my writing. She didn't need any freelance services because she had just hired a full-time, senior-level writer.

I may be able to bring in some money by composing and editing documents for other people's job hunts. This is an online gig where I'd be given the job hunter's current resume and a few other documents that help in the writing, editing, and design. I tried a fake job—one that is just for practice—but I neglected to call the resume editing service manager who was assigned to my case before creating the new resume and putting it on this outfit's Website. I called her to let her know what I had done. She thought I was being argumentative as she acted like I had done some sort of cardinal and deadly sin. I was just trying to explain that the instructions were a little unclear, and oh boy, did that ever set her off! She challenged me to not raise a fuss until I was running my own company. In the end, she laughed a destructive, cynical, and snide laugh into my ear as the call ended.

My depression came back. The parasitic worm got drunk off my juices and danced around in my head, singing off key to the tune of "Suicide Is Painless."

The net result was that I just put the idea aside for future consideration. There has to be a better way to make a living than sucking up to an Internet company for assignments geared to finding a job for some other schmuck. But now, as the money situation becomes more serious, perhaps I will give that outfit another try—after the holidays. Yes, after the craziness, over-consumption, family feuding, and all the other pressures of creating a good time pass, in pain, like calcified kidney stones.

When I think about our situation within these lights, I become more hopeful. I am a successful freelance writer, if getting a book written and published over a period of nine months means anything. I was a technical computer guy when I was working full time, and the book is about computers. It compiles a lot of information about and insight into large storage systems: disk drive arrays, automated tape silos, automated backups, and disaster recovery, among other subjects.

I thought doing such a work would help in the job hunt, but just the opposite has occurred. Headhunters tell me not to mention the book to prospective employers. I don't understand why. Are employers afraid of writers? If so, why do they insist that their prospective employees have excellent communication skills? Maybe they are afraid I'll write something bad about their companies. If they are doing something crooked like WorldCom, Enron, Global Crossing, and the rest of the companies in trouble now for past transgressions, I don't blame them. But come on, all I want to do is support some big computers and make some decent money. I don't care what shenanigans are going on in the upper management ranks. That's why I have never wanted to be a manager, get it? Nor do I want to become a mud-raking journalist, although with this behavior being shown about my book, I am starting to consider the career alternative. What are these employers afraid of?

Another way to look at this is that employers really don't want to hire people who can think at the levels high enough to write a commercially published book. They just want people who can write well enough to do status reports for upper management that avoid the use of any technical terms and don't have any big words in them.

This situation has always made me leery of upper management. Are they really that uniformed about their business? Are they really that illiterate? You know, after reviewing hundreds of university student papers, many from currently working managers, I do think the high ranks of business management are often filled by complete idiots. Still, I have personally known many very sharp business managers. It just amazes me that some managers of technology companies don't know about the technologies that are sold, and therefore bring in the money that eventually goes into their bonus checks.

Admittedly, technical terms are sometimes hard to understand, but anyone can do an Internet search on the terms and discover what they mean.

Do you suppose some of these bad managers don't know how to use the Internet? Anyway, I've written this book, see? And it is a good book. So gimme a goddamn job, okay? Oh, I know what you're thinking: With an attitude like this, why would anyone want to give me a job? Well, I'm not stupid and job hunting isn't new to me. I'll write about my bad attitude here, but when it comes to interviewing, I follow all the guidelines. You know, all the things that make job interviews total bullshit. The tricks, the counter-tricks, the misunderstandings, the prejudices, the—well, listing all this just gets me riled up.

I think we ought to just skip Christmas. I mean, what good is it? People overspend on junk nobody really wants, get depressed, burn a bunch of electricity with house lights (which I happen to enjoy looking at, by the way), overeat, fight with each other, get further depressed, and then celebrate the phony birthday of a savior. We sure as hell need one after all that.

I'm going to contradict myself here. I really like Christmas, at least some parts of it. This is the time of year that I study carols arranged for guitar and other music in the classical vein. Christmas has inspired some mighty fine tunes. "Winter Wonderland" is one of my favorites this year.

Why not celebrate winter solstice and just be done with it? If you want to throw Jesus a birthday bash, go ahead— nobody's going to try to stop you. The First Amendment does give you the right to celebrate your religion any way you see fit, as long as you aren't crashing jet liners into skyscrapers or killing little kids and the such. Killing chickens might be all right though. And Kosher killing is okay. Just don't get carried away with drinking the blood of the lamb, if you know what I mean.

Lydia (she's my "significant other," or as I like to use, "sigoth," pronounced "sig'-awth") is a bah-humbugger to the extreme. She would like to skip Christmas, and she would like to get reimbursement from all her former Christmases, too. She'd like her step-father to not have killed himself on Christmas day all those years ago, and to not have had her sister keel over from a brain aneurism on that same fateful day in the calendar. So you can imagine the mood in this house right now. We aren't exactly fa-lah-lah-ing, gaily decked out while dashing through snow. Colorado is in a drought right now, so there isn't any dang snow to dash through, even if we wanted to.

I don't know. We seem to be dealing with too many things at once. If it isn't terrorism, it's war with Iraq. If it isn't money problems, it is old baggage from holidays past. At least we don't have little kids to take care of, and I feel for those who do. Maybe people will be skipping Christmas this year but not on purpose. Maybe the Grinch wins this one.

Well, enough about Christmas and unemployment. This is the first time in my life that I've been unemployed over two consecutive Christmases. That sucks. There, I am now officially done with this particular angle on the subjects.

I can give a little advice to others who have been unemployed for a long time, or even a short time. For one thing, you need to keep busy. Sitting around the house steeped in depression is the most damaging thing you can do to yourself. Worrying about money isn't good either, but I understand how this is always a concern, and I really have no idea how to get rid of that worry. We have been conditioned to consume.

Conditioned to consume, we get depressed when our past consumption comes back in the form of credit card bills. Then we get depressed when we can't consume any longer, except for the bare necessities of life. The news keeps harping at us to spend more money, and gee whiz, I sure would like to accommodate that requirement of economic recovery. But you see, I'm an unemployed bum who has to live off of my sigoth's generosity. So forget it: My consumer confidence is shot to hell.

Anyway, you need to keep busy. Career development is something you can work on while unemployed. Hey, maybe you can fit into alternative career paths with what you have. I mean, if I could move from a warehouse job to a computer job back in the late 1970s, maybe you can move from your old computer career into …, well, maybe into nothing. No! Stop! We can't think that way. Grab that juice-sucking worm and fling it away.

Here's a Website that is a good starting place for career development:

http://www.jobhuntersbible.com/

I used the main book mentioned on this site, *What Color Is Your Parachute*, when I made the career move from working class to professional computer guy. The idea is that you have skills and talents that can fit into several different career paths. First, you need to identify your strongest skills and talents. Then you need to figure out what career paths these skills and talents would fit into. Finally, you need to network to find opportunities to pursue your selected career path.

I talk a good talk on this subject because I've used *Parachute* techniques all throughout my computer career. The first move from the warehouse was into technical writing. I knew I could write, had a lot of credits toward an English major, and knew quite a bit about mechanics, electronics, chemistry, and various other sciences. What I needed to learn about whatever technology, I could learn. In college I had learned how to learn and to become a lifelong learner—before being a lifelong learner was cool.

While seeking out a specific target for technical writing, I discovered that the computer industry had moved rather quickly ahead since I had been in college. This looked like a growth industry, and so I went about pursuing a technical writing job within it.

The first thing I did was to do all those exercises in *Parachute*. You need to write five or so stories about things you've done in your life that made you proud, gave you pleasure, or in some other ways made your life enjoyable. Then you go through the stories to pick out the skills and talents that you used when doing these things.

From there, you build a skills inventory to use as part of your self-promotion into your chosen career direction. But how do you pick a direction? Two main ways you go about doing this are:

Talk to people. Ask them opinions on what career directions are or will be good ones to follow. You may get a lot of opinions that aren't very reliable, ideas that seem too strange to consider, or a lot of blank looks. If you are doing cold-calling, you will also experience rejection, runarounds, and brush-offs. Although this isn't any fun, the experiences will prepare you for your job hunt networking efforts.

Explore what the government has to say about industries and careers. When we are working, we pay a lot of federal taxes. Some of this money goes into studies done by the Department of Labor. The *Parachute* Website mentioned above discusses what's available to you through the government, along with many other sources of career selection information, and even some exercises to help in the decision-making process.

One thing to always keep in mind: The more focused and directed you are, the better the chance that you will eventually find a position in line with your career goals. When people finally do talk with you, this energy will beam on through your eyes, and if you're into psychic things, your aura. You will have enthusiasm written all over you.

The trouble with what has been going on during this recession is that hardly anyone is hiring, and those who are hiring are very picky. I frankly have never seen it this bad, so not being able to find a job is something a lot of us are dealing with. Lydia keeps telling me that I do have a job, and that job is writing while I keep tabs on the job market for fifty-year-old systems administrators.

Over the past year, I've had a grand total of four interviews, all but one with IBM up in Boulder, about a hundred miles from our little place in Woodland Park. I've pushed my rather extensive resume out to hundreds of openings without much success, and the news is full of stories about employers getting thousands of resumes for a single opening. This wasn't out of the ordinary during past recessions—it's just that this one seems to be especially elongated. You know the reasons, too. Massive bad, and even illegal, business practices have shrunk the job market worse than immersion in icy water shrinks male genitalia.

And now, with the push for war on Iraq, the stagnant job market doesn't seem to have any hope for improvement anytime soon. So, I can give job hunting advice until I'm blue in the face, yet I can't find a job myself. One news report that came over the radio had to do with a newly laid off employment counselor. He said that he sat down in front of his home computer and asked himself, "Now what? I've always given advice on finding jobs—but I've never had to go find a job myself!"

Well, I have had to find jobs for myself, and as most will report, this is a lot more work than performing in the actual job. Freelance writing is like this too—you put in a lot of time researching, writing, rewriting, researching more, rewriting, and onward until you have something that might sell. Then you have to sell the work to a publisher. Eventually, you might get a royalty check. Let's just say that I'm very, very appreciative of Lydia. Without her, I'd have been run down by that iron ore train long ago.

That's another thing about unemployment: It can ruin your marriage, relationship, or whatever you have for economic and emotional support. I'll admit that sometimes I can be a real asshole and Lydia can be a real bitch. Men are from the planet Proctos, and women are from the planet Canine. Don't hedge this with nice, airy-fairy pseudo-psych. We can destroy a lot of what we've worked toward with our loved ones once the pressure is on. My advice? I don't know. Good luck. We've lived through a lot and have a lot more to live through before this is done. Somehow we've managed to not hurt each other to the point of no return, but we've come close. At times, living out of the Jeep has seemed like an attractive alternative to living with a bitch. Lydia has, at times, considered this to be a good way for me to go as well.

I suppose I can advise that you keep on talking with your mate. Talking helps. Being honest with your feelings helps. I mean, I've not been angry with Lydia as much as the smarmy, greedy, dishonest pricks who run good companies into the ground. Taking some time to play loud blues music in the basement while tooting harmonica helps me. You might want to give that a whirl.

~ *3* ~

Born Under a Bad Sign

I woke up this morning with a realization that I have lost everything three other times in my life: after college, after the bankruptcy of StorageTek and the subsequent depression that hit Colorado in the 1980s, and after the breakup in Memphis from Laurel, whom I lived with for about six years. Looks like a pattern, and some of you may be thinking that I must be doing something wrong. Well, maybe I was simply born at the wrong time.

I have three siblings who are all older than me: Ruby Anne was born in 1938, Rick in 1945, and Rolph in 1947. I was born in 1952. Rubes (as the family calls her) married shortly out of high school and started having babies. In 1956, she moved with her family to California where she finished raising her kids, retired, and now lives with her retired spouse, Ernest (Sooky, as the family calls him), near the coast of Oregon. Rick went to Vietnam, returned, and worked in the iron mines of Northern Minnesota until he retired early at the age of 55, two years ago. Rollie, as we called him, joined the National Guard to avoid the Vietnam draft of 1966, and did a similar thing as Rick— worked in the iron mines until he drew disability and died in 1998 at the age of 51.

In 1970, when I graduated from high school and was seeking work in the iron mines like my brothers, the economy went into an 11-month business "contraction," as the National Bureau of Economic Research calls it when jobs are tough to find. I did find a fair job as a parts picker with a heavy equipment firm, but nine months later I was laid off. With job prospects looking bad, I went to college. This also gave me a draft deferment, but I really didn't need one because the 1971 draft lottery gave me a high number.

In 1975, I left college; and in 1975, another business contraction started that lasted three months. I ended up being a motorcycle mechanic making a little over minimum wage.

I wasn't off to a very good start, economically, in life. At least I didn't need to take out student loans for college, so working for the low wages wasn't so bad. However, I wasn't making enough to buy any real estate: not a house, condo, or anything. Then, in 1979, things started to look up—I got a break into technical writing in the computer field.

Three years later, in 1982, I decided to try freelance technical writing. Another economic contraction started then and lasted for 11 months. This time I did have toys to abandon but not very many. I remember leaving a pair of cross-country skis behind, a very nice traditional set made from ash. That, and a couple of monster stereo speakers.

The Christmas season of 1982 saw me heading to Colorado for a job promised over the phone. When I arrived, I had only 10 dollars left and no absolutely solid job offer. As it turned out, the job with StorageTek did come through. Whew!

Three years later, StorageTek went into Chapter 11 bankruptcy. I and a large number of techies were laid off, which flooded the Colorado job market. Colorado went into a lengthy contraction due to the oil and gas industries having hard times. After frantically searching for work, Federal Express offered me a job in Memphis, Tennessee.

The economy remained fairly stable, so I felt confident taking a different job in 1988. I moved from Tennessee to Virginia where I worked for five years with three different companies. The first job ended after about two years. I had automated myself out of a mainframe systems programming position. You see, my primary responsibilities involved monitoring a system and producing reports from historical records. Using a combination of assembler, SAS, REXX, and GDDM, I created programs that did all of this for me—and so, I was rewarded with a $16,000 dollar severance (not too bad for the time) and a chance to "explore other career paths," as we who are terminally optimistic tend to think.

The second job was a 1099 contract that lasted 12 months, and the third was with a regional bank. Then MCI hired me to work in Colorado. This led to a six-year period of career growth and expansion into Unix systems administration. With the economy going quite strong in 1999, I took a job with a local hospital to support their Unix systems and bring them through the great Year 2000 scare. Then I went back to MCI, which had been bought by WorldCom, as a highly paid contractor. I was at my peak of income at over $78,000 a year. A couple of years earlier, Lydia and I bought this house together.

This house isn't anything fancy, but it is in the mountains and has a nice view of Pikes Peak. We bought it for the view. Feeling confident that the new Information Age economy was defying all previous economic models, we began some remodeling efforts. We had the front entrance deck and stairs ripped out, redesigned, and renewed. This house is now twenty-two years old. It had the original decking when we bought it, and that decking was rotting from age. It became downright unsafe. We also had the kitchen remodeled because that usually adds value to the house.

Then, in November of 2001, my contract with WorldCom was not renewed. Hopeful predictions for 2002 economic recovery came and went. More techies were laid off nationwide. WorldCom went into bankruptcy, as did several other major employers.

As I look over my career and life choices, I've made mistakes, good moves, and been simply a victim of circumstances. What can I say to people other than you try your best and reach for the highest lot in life you can, and sometimes you get caught in the headlamps? I know my iron ore mining brothers went through harsh times in the 1980s as the rust belt jobs came under fire. I know my sister and her family have gone through hard times. My point is not that I'm whining about my lot in life, just that a pattern of getting hit by economic contraction has been my lot. I'm simply asking for less judgment from my fellow human beings. I'd also like a few more breaks from whatever positive spirits might be available to me.

The thing is though, I could be heading toward a lucrative career as a writer of technical and other books—like this one. Wouldn't that be something? What if my guitar playing matures to where I actually get a recording contract, or link up with others for recording various things? The good thing about being caught in the headlamps is that something knocks off half your pride, throws you in the snow bank, and as some asshole tries to saw your nuts off with a dull blade, you get to kick the crap out of him. I don't like fighting like this, but put yourself in my place. Wouldn't you rebel, even just a little? Wouldn't you carry a chip on your shoulder, maybe just a little one the size of a toothpick? Well, maybe the size of a two-by-four. Yeah, an oak two-by-four just for assholes like Gabby with his dull knife, sawing away with a shit-eating grin on his face. Well, that's the feeling, anyway. I don't really beat anyone up, and so I get to deal with a lot of swallowed anger, and that leads to depression, and then we've got to figure out how to move forward.

Some people go through life following a career defined by others: Career directions are chosen not because they please you, but because that's where the money is. I think this is a wrong way to do it. You should follow what you are inherently good at and figure out how these talents can be used within the context of a job. Generally speaking, you enjoy what you are good at. I enjoy writing so much that when the ideas aren't flowing, I'm off on Internet political boards yakking away on things I know little about. Oh what the heck, everyone is doing it. Very little knowledge has never stopped anyone, even professional politicians, from talking endlessly on any particular subject. Just take a look at our present crop of politicians in Colorado—complete imbeciles when it comes to planned growth, public transportation, wildfire management, social problems like drug use and abuse, and just about anything that comes to the table. We don't hire our politicians for their level of intelligence, that is obvious. If you go by the writings of Mark Twain and Will Rogers, we never have.

However that shakes out, my oldest brother thought I ought to major in business administration while in college. That's where the money is, he'd argue. Yeah, and what if I told you that I absolutely hate that idea? Do you suppose I'd get good grades? Enjoy anything about my job later on? Probably not. So I started out majoring in biology.

Now that's a kicker, isn't it? Why biology? Well, I also enjoy working with things like the periodic table and examining how life itself works. The sciences have always been an attraction, and even to this day I like reading about new discoveries in most of the sciences. Except psychology, that is. I'm not sure anything new is to be discovered—but that's just me.

Along the way, a couple of English professors suggested

that I major in English. I settled upon that for the undergraduate work because dissecting sentences, paragraphs, short stories, novels, and deep thoughts isn't as messy as dissecting animals. I like reading about biology more than doing it. The same goes for paleontology, sociology, physics, chemistry, and higher math. The only straight application of science I truly enjoy is motorcycle mechanics, and a whole book has been written on the Zen of that. Yet I hate the idea of engineering motorcycles—or anything else for that matter. When you add all this up and try to figure out a career path, technical writing comes immediately to mind, if you know what technical writers do. Back in the warehouse days, I didn't even know such people existed, although I had read plenty of technical manuals on motorcycles. I just never thought that someone might be paid to make these things.

Later on in my tech writing career, I found myself producing hardware documentation for an architecture and modeling group of engineers. Here's where I learned about *queuing theory mathematics*, a discipline that attempts to forecast the performance of computing systems based on how services are rendered and how *queues*, or lines of things waiting for the services, form. The classic example of a system that can be described this way is a barber shop. You only have so many barbers; they can cut hair only so fast; as a result, customers queue up for their haircuts. You can shorten the queues by adding more barbers, making the barbers more efficient, or reducing the demand for haircuts (least desirable). This analogy maps directly to how computers work: when programs run, demand builds for services like CPU cycles, memory, input/output and so forth. If the services can't satisfy demand right away, the demand forms a queue, or lines up like customers waiting for haircuts.

Our manager, Chuck, had a habit of kicking a packing corner off one of our metal bookshelves that poked out into the aisle between cubicle rows. The packing corner was used for shipping the big computing machinery of the day: It had a three-sided plastic molding with a bright yellow plastic donut glued on—for absorbing shock. We had decorated our ugly, battleship gray bookshelf with two of these packing corners. Chuck always kicked one of the corners off, which shot across the area, right after his management staff meeting. It was his way of letting off steam as StorageTek headed toward Chapter 11 bankruptcy, and the worst behaviors of humans caught in the headlamps came into play.

One day I was playing with an idea and presented it to the engineers. What if we hooked the two packing corners together using paper clips and rubber bands? Make it so that Chuck wouldn't see the setup. Then, the next time Chuck kicked—

The engineers loved the idea, and so we did it. The next time Chuck kicked, the two corners flopped flaccidly together. His satisfaction had been foiled! We all laughed uproariously. After Chuck regained composure, he asked who had come up with this bright idea, in a sarcastic tone. I volunteered my guilt in the matter, and a few weeks later, Chuck recommended me for mainframe systems programming training. He had recognized the latent engineer in me who didn't want to design plastic corners, only make them do things out of the ordinary.

I feel sorry for the folks trying to build a career these days. Tough times have brought the most terrible hiring practices I have ever witnessed. The Internet has delivered tremendous value, but it has also enabled automated screening programs that plop you into narrowly defined categories like a sorting machine at a Federal Express package hub. We are no longer a human being, and we are worse than a number. We are commodities to be sorted and delivered, or sorted and rejected. If you are lucky enough to land a job, you probably won't advance as easily as I did, relatively speaking, with Chuck's help. People like Chuck seem to have left the building, retired to the country, or been abducted by aliens. At least the aliens recognize solid management practices. Maybe Chuck is working on that new generation of flying saucer? Maybe he's doing crop circles for kicks? I don't know, but he sure helped me out when help was needed.

Right now we haven't lost everything. We are keeping up with house payments, utilities, and Lydia's credit bills. She still has a few thousand dollars left in her retirement account, and we will use that money for survival if necessary. No, this isn't like the time in Memphis, after breaking up with Laurel, when all I had was an old station wagon, a sleeping bag, a few furnishings, and a guitar. Oh yes, and a .357 magnum Ruger revolver that was once owned by my father. That Christmas, I considered eating a bullet because depression had hit me so badly. Fortunately, the old movie, *It's A Wonderful Life*, came on as I was practicing my final meal of hot lead with an empty revolver. Click! Just like that, click and gone. No more pain. No more anticipation of a big, steam-driven iron ore train smashing me down. No more feelings of failure or whatever those emotions are when a relationship breaks apart.

Anger? Well, yeah, anger. But toward what? Nobody was really to blame; things just didn't work out. Hatred? No, I didn't hate Laurel. I was disappointed a lot, but I didn't wish her harm. All I knew was that I felt more miserable than at any other time in my life, and I wanted that misery to end.

I had never seen the movie before. It caught my attention, so I put away the revolver and made some popcorn. The snowy early scenes reminded me of Minnesota, Johnny, deer camp, and my parent's generation. They never ate bullets when the times turned tough. They put one foot in front of the other and moved on.

The George Bailey character reminded me of myself—always wanting to leave my stinking little hometown. The Mary Hatch character reminded me of my high school sweetheart, Mary Kay. Everyone thought we'd get married after she graduated. I was a year older, had already graduated, and needed desperately to get out to see the world, or as much of it as I could. So I broke it off with Mary Kay, rather abruptly too because, you see, nobody ever talked about much in my hometown. Not about anything that might be important, anyway. I've always felt badly about not explaining things to her first. All I could come up with was that I didn't love her enough for marriage—but the real thing was that I had no idea what the hell love was, and I was just scared.

So George Bailey hangs around his small town while others go off with their lives. He falls in love with Mary Hatch, who loved him all along. Right there I thought, hey, this is my story had I married Mary Kay! Then the story moves along to where George thinks about killing himself. Man, very close stuff, downright spooky how close. Along comes Clarence, the angel, and the eventual happy ending where you bawl your eyes out almost every time.

I bought the video shortly afterward and a VCR to play it. For years that movie kept me going when times turned tough. I only watch it maybe once a year now. I've pretty much memorized the whole thing.

Lydia and I are still friendly with Dick, her ex-husband. His favorite movie is *It's A Wonderful Life* too. He likes to ride motorcycle and play bagpipes—Scottish blood. Dick has also needed to declare bankruptcy some years back. Life is sometimes so ironic that it resembles bad fiction.

Apparently, if you can survive certain periods of life, life does get better. Then it gets bad again, but now you know more about getting out of the frozen trance as the headlamps bear down.

My survival instinct is pretty strong. I've been in several very tight situations that could have easily cost my life, but by putting one foot in front of the other and taking things as they come, with a constant prayer for help from anyone—God, Jesus, Buddha, Allah, Krishna, The Great Spirit, Clarence— going on in my head, I somehow pulled through, and this was always with the help of some kind, and sometimes not so kind, souls.

Back in April of 1995, I got a bug up my rear to get a dual-sport motorcycle. I'd been working steady for many years, and so my credit was in excellent shape. A call to a motorcycle shop confirmed that several models of dual-sports were available. The dual-sport motorcycle is one that's designed for both highway and dirt trail use. The one I picked was more for the highway than dirt, but it handled well enough in the dirt for what I wanted to do. So I bought a Suzuki DR650, an air-cooled, single-cylinder, 650cc displacement bike. The stock Harleys of today displace about 1300cc, so I figured the DR650 was half a Harley.

The bike stood pretty tall. The shop guy that set it up wanted to top it off with gas before I took possession. When the shop guy mounted the bike, he had to take a leap up into the saddle, almost as if this was a horse and not a machine.

For the next few weeks, I rode the DR650 around town and up a moderately rough mountain road called Rampart Range Road, from Colorado Springs, where I was living at the time in a junky old apartment. Snow still covered Rampart Range

Road at its higher reaches, so I could only go part way up before turning back.

Then in May, the snow went away, and I trekked farther and farther up into the hills. For each excursion, I carried a backpack full of survival supplies like fire starters, food bars, water, water purification tablets, rain gear, and the .357 Ruger. In addition, I carried insulated overalls.

Rampart Range Road goes from the Garden of the Gods in Colorado Springs all the way up to a paved county road not too far from Deckers. Some miles before the county road, I found a bunch of trails for motorcycles. It was a bright spring day, and I was feeling like a little more challenge in the dirt, so I tried one of the single-track trails.

The first one wasn't too bad. It got steep here and there, but it eventually came out to a two-track forest road, and I took that back up to Rampart Range Road. With my first success, I tried a mild-looking trail on the other side. This one tricked me.

Almost right away, I had to go down a steep grade that I knew I couldn't get back up—not with the half-assed stock tires that came with the DR650. The next challenge was a creek crossing, and even though I negotiated it well enough, I knew I wanted an easier trail.

I came upon a crossroad. Going to the right, I encountered another creek crossing. Turning around and going back to the crossroad, I tried another leg. A big tree had fallen over it, too big to jump, so I tried the last alternative at the crossroad. This one seemed good as it gently descended toward what I thought might be another forest road.

The trail turned into a narrow rock shelf with some stair-step formations I had to navigate. I knew then that I would not be going back this way either. Although the grade was within my and the DR650's abilities, those stair-steps were much too hairy to do uphill. Even going downhill gave me deep-gut vertigo as I tried to ignore the steep fall to my left and concentrated on the wall side of the shelf trail.

The trail did not bring me to the forest road I had hoped to find, but to the widest, deepest creek crossing I'd ever seen. The trail widened out to a gravely area, so I stopped the DR650, shut her down, and dismounted to look over the area and crossing. It was about two o'clock in the afternoon. I still had five or six hours before sunset.

Something caught my eye in the gravel. It was a set of motorcycle front forks, the tire up in the air. I pushed on the tire a little and realized that almost a whole dirt motorcycle was buried in the gravel! It must have been missing its rear wheel because there was no sign of that, and by the angle of the forks, it should have been visible too. Whatever the condition of the bike, this was not a good sign.

Checking out the creek crossing, I gazed over rapidly moving brown water. The spring rains had been heavy, and the melt-off of winter snows was well underway. The creek looked like it might be too deep, and the other side was a good thirty feet away.

I walked up and down the creek bank, searching for alternatives to crossing. Dense brush stopped any idea of riding the bank to a forest road one way, and the other way the bank ran right into a rock wall. I had no choice but to try a creek crossing, so I waded out into the water to check its force and depth.

The water came up to my lower thighs, probably around three feet deep. The force wasn't too bad right at the crossing. Returning to the DR650, I checked the water depth as marked on my jeans to the height of the spark plug and air intake. I had around six inches to spare. Yep, I thought to myself, this is worth a try.

Mounting my bike, I fired it up and let the engine get good and warm. Easing to the creek bank in first gear, I took a deep breath and started out slowly, giving it just a little gas, angling upstream. I actually made it to the other side before the rear wheel spun and dug into the creek bed as I tried to get up the slight rise of the opposite bank. That was enough digging to bring the engine completely under the water, wetting the sparkplug, and killing my power.

Damn, I thought, *so close!* I'd have to push it the rest of the way, but first I needed to unload my survival gear and toss it on the bank. I had almost finished this task when the side stand lost its footing in the creek bed, and the DR650 slipped sideways downstream into deeper and faster water. I hung onto the bike with a stretching bungee chord. The bike slipped farther downstream, pulling me along. When I was almost chest-deep in water, the bike no longer visible, I let go of the bungee chord.

Although I've loved and lost several times in my life, this feeling of loss was devastating. I stared at the water for a solid minute, feeling like I had just abandoned a good friend without enough fight—that I should have hung on to the bitter end. Looking back on this, it was a pretty stupid feeling, but at the time I couldn't help it.

I slopped myself back to my survival equipment to take inventory. I had three liters of water, five energy bars, some crackers, fire starters, knife, insulated coverall, empty thermos that once held creamed and sugared coffee, and rain suit. Yep, enough to find my way out.

Here's where I made a mistake. I decided to keep going along the trail instead of back the way I had come. I was convinced this trail would come out to a forest road that I could take back to Rampart Range Road and flag down a ride to town.

What I found was another creek crossing, deeper and faster than the last, and a long uphill climb that I couldn't finish before sunset. I camped on the hillside that night before a small fire of dead fall branches, my father's .357 magnum laid across my lap clad in the dry insulated coveralls, my wet jeans drying nearby.

Sleep came in fits that night. I was warm enough in the coveralls, and the jeans eventually dried. As the black night turned to a gray dawn, I shouldered my backpack and took up the trail again.

By noon I had come to the top of a ridge and another crossroad. My senses told me to go to the left. This way brought me to a small creek where I refilled my water jugs and used water purification tablets to ward off the nasties associated with untreated mountain water: giardia and others.

Shortly thereafter, the trail eventually came to a wide forest road, and judging by the bright spot in the overcast skies, I took the way that led east, back to Rampart Range Road. It was about one o'clock in the afternoon. A half hour later, I heard the unmistakable sounds of four-stroke engines.

Three ATVs came over a hill toward me. Riding them was a father, a son, and a hired hand who worked for the father's church in some mountain town—Pine maybe. I forget. The father asked me what I was doing out in the middle of nowhere, and I explained what had happened. He asked me where my map was. I admitted that I had no map, just a very good sense of direction and the lay of land and roads. After shaking his pious head and commenting how I reminded him of his brother, obviously someone who has not earned his place in heaven, he offered me a ride to Sedalia, a little town north of Colorado Springs. I accepted the offer.

That ATV ride was one of the wildest I've ever had. The

good reverend was getting his kicks before returning to his flock. I had to lean and duck branches all the way back to their pickup truck and trailer. Rain started to fall as we loaded up the ATVs and headed to Sedalia.

The reverend dropped me off at a bar/café, and I thanked him for his trouble. I offered to pitch in a couple of bucks for gas, but he would have none of that. His good deed was sufficient for him. In retrospect, I should have offered the money as a donation to his church! Ah well, guess my guardian angel knew something I did not.

So there you go. I was very lucky or my prayers were answered. It seems that some people can go through life without much challenge—physically, intellectually, and emotionally. Or so it seems. I imagine everyone gets their share of stress and challenge in this life. So, I guess I shouldn't complain, but I do anyway.

Do you feel that every time you get your shit together, life comes along and kicks you in the teeth? Or do you live in constant anxiety on the railroad tracks, knowing that some iron ore train is bound to come roaring down on you? Well, brothers and sisters, you aren't alone on this one. I've had psychics tell me that the more troubles you have in life, the more you grow spiritually. I suppose so. I mean, look at Jesus Christ's life. Now there's a guy who had a boatload of problems, but things eventually turned out. Or look at Buddha's life—nothing seemed to be working out for him until his Enlightenment.

So maybe, just maybe, I was born under an extremely good sign.

~ *4* ~
Scraping for a Living

Lydia just contacted my bankruptcy lawyer to start her own process of stiffing unsecured loan creditors. The university she teaches for has cut her pay in half. Her credit card companies have raised her interest rates, probably because so many people are declaring bankruptcy these days. I know the feelings she is going through: defeat, depression, anxiety, self-doubt, despair, glimmering hope, and backsliding into darkness. The iron ore train roars on, its headlamps causing paralysis of mind. Panic! Run! Move! But you can't.

The longest I've been out of a job up until now was two months. It seemed like, even during the darkest of times previously experienced, there were pockets of hiring going on. Jobs were somewhere, and one of my survival strategies was to rent apartments rather than pursue real estate in the form of a condo or house. This allowed for rapid movement from state to state in pursuit of jobs. Now, being a homeowner and partnered with Lydia, I don't have the option to move out of state even if jobs were available elsewhere. We have considered what it would take for me to work long-distance, but none of the options make much sense. The additional income to the household would not be enough to turn the corner, to jump the tracks and head back into the gentle starlight, away from the screaming light of the headlamps. What would happen is we'd double our living costs, and I would not be here with Lydia. Both of us would get lonesome, she'd have to figure out how to get the driveway cleared if it snowed, and I'd be away from my writing nook.

Lydia has been drumming up income through teaching online classes and reviewing student papers. This looks like the best course for now, but I have additional plans once the holiday season of 2002 passes and the new year of 2003 commences. I'll be cold-calling for freelance writing jobs, researching for books on other subjects, helping Lydia with the classes and editing chores, and continuing my job hunt aggressively.

Over the first year of unemployment, I have learned that the Internet has worked to my disadvantage. Jobs posted on the Net attract hundreds, perhaps thousands, of applicants each. It is too easy to fire off emails to apply for jobs, and worse, agents that automatically blast resumes all over the place exist. A lot of scams or questionable service organizations have cropped up to take some of your savings, some of your severance pay, or some of your unemployment compensation. The resume has become a cheaper document that it formerly was. An email resume is becoming almost the same as junk email, or as known in the email world, *spam*. Why is it called spam? Apparently this was derived from a Monty Python sketch that made fun of the meat product called Spam. The job hunt process often seems like a bad Monty Python sketch as people's behaviors turn strange under stress.

It is true that I have had a few telephone interviews as a result of submitting my resume by email. My skills are still viable in the job market, but the market doesn't have enough jobs available. Employers have become very picky because they can afford to wait for the absolutely perfect candidate—or the more likely explanation, the candidate who interviews the best. The hiring process has always been a soft science. Often, it is the feeling around a candidate rather than experience or credentials that carries the most weight in the decision-making process.

Telephone interviews are killers, especially the interviews that are done by several people gathered around a speaker phone.

Back when I was transitioning from the parts picker position to technical writer in computers (1979), I learned that you can't do this through resumes. In fact, the outfit that did finally hire me had rejected my resume a few weeks before because I had no technical writing experience. What brought me to the position was a network of people whom I contacted through cold-calling. I knew I would make a good tech writer because I wrote well (English major) and liked to do my own mechanical and electrical maintenance on cars and motorcycles. This argument went well with the hiring manager who had picked a tech writer for the position, but she quit a week later after her former employer offered more money. The hiring manager needed a replacement quick, and one who would stick around for a while. He also liked motorcycles.

The cold-calling went like this: First, I called a couple of people who were cold fish. One even told me that my cold-call was very annoying and why don't I just send his company a resume. I said, "Well, sir, I don't have any experience as a technical writer." The guy laughed in my ear. Then, I talked with a tech writing manager with Honeywell who granted an interview.

I asked her some prepared questions about what the job of technical writer involved, and then she looked deeply into my eyes and asked if I was certain I wanted to become one of these overworked and seldom-thanked people. She must have seen something in my eyes because she then directed me to the STC (Society of Technical Communicators) and one of the organization's officers. This guy told me about the hiring manager who needed someone quickly, and the job came from that last interview with the hiring manager. After the interview, he showed off his panhead Harley chopper, a beauty in chrome and black.

Something has happened though, over the decades. I've been having a harder time building a contact network this time around. Nobody has wanted to talk with me from the viewpoint of a Unix systems administrator, and I suspect this is due to corporate policies that restrict employees from talking to anyone outside the organization. After all, I could be a writer, and I could write an article, and the article may be critical of the corporation.

I can understand this fear. I am a writer. Writers, by their natures and perhaps by some kind of unstated code of ethics, must be honest in their writings. Otherwise, you are a propagandist and therefore untrustworthy. Judging from all the dirt that has come out about certain corporations over the past year, I understand this reluctance to talk with outsiders, especially writers.

How long can this situation go on? Will it only get worse as we categorize people into arbitrary niches while ignoring unique traits of the individual? It seems to me that a concerted effort has been going on since the 1980s to undo, unravel, and disintegrate the notion of the individual in favor of the compartmentalizing and commoditizing of individuals. We are either college graduates or we are not. Life experience does not count for much. Transferable skills don't seem to matter. Inherent abilities, such as writing, that have been trained into the discipline of a professional count less than the ability to format documents using exactly the software in use, at least for technical writers. This has been especially discouraging as I seek out any job that would fit.

Please don't take me wrong: I am not arguing against the value of a college education, but now it has become an arbitrary requirement for many positions. Some organizations do still consider equitable life experience, but how do you, in two words or less, explain that your undergraduate degree is only about sixteen credits short? How do you give a plausible explanation as to how you came to be a professional (or at least nearly professional) writer without that BA in English?

One paranoid thought I have about this is that if the high-tech workers of the United States can be reduced to commodities like sacks of coffee or sugar, foreign high-tech workers can more easily be imported under H-1B visas. Granted, lots of requirements surround the granting of an H-1B visa, and hopefully the government and corporations are being careful who gets visas and under what conditions. I'd hate to find out that visas have been granted to put Americans out of work. Sometimes I suspect that Americans are not given breaks into certain positions because the learning curve would be too long, and an H-1B visa person, most likely from India, is chosen instead due to a perceived status that may or may not be true. Many unemployed high-tech workers, citizens of the United States of America, very probably loyal Republican voters, have expressed these concerns through technical forums, emails, and letters to editors. After the recent corporate scandals and lack of oversight by the Securities and Exchange Commission, I do wonder how much rule-stretching goes on with the Department of Labor. I often feel that my government is working against the interests of its citizens. Perhaps high-tech workers were making too much money during the boom times in the 1990s. Perhaps wealth was distributing downward at an alarming rate.

This memory comes strongly to mind: In 2000, a high school dropout took a programming job with WorldCom. His starting wage? Sixty thousand dollars a year. That's what I was making at the hospital with two decades of experience!

Well, that was three years ago. A lot can change over three years. No wonder we freeze up in the headlamps, and is that a sneering engineer's face I see? Is a band of cynical, disloyal, money-grubbing capitalists stoking up the fires of the ore train's boiler? Or is it just that, like Sandy Makinnen, they just don't care at all? Who will get us off these tracks? Can we do it ourselves?

An interesting irony comes out of all this. Currently, and for the foreseeable future, Lydia and I are keeping our heads above water because many people have decided to pursue their college degrees or to add a graduate degree to their resumes. This has increased demand for online education, and so the University of Phoenix has enjoyed an increase in business. Fear of the future in others is keeping us going.

I'm trying very hard to consider what I do each day as work. It just doesn't have regular paydays, weekends, vacations, or benefits like health insurance. Yet, if I don't do something toward writing books, marketing the published book, or finding a new job, then I feel that the day is a complete waste. It has become extremely hard to relax and take a break.

Back when I was doing a 1099 gig for Xerox, I did much of my work from home. Defining the workday became a problem as I'd put in a lot more hours that usual. Eventually, I learned how to set a time to start and stop so that I could get out of the apartment every now and then to smell the roses and run errands. That's not the problem this time around—what both of us have a hard time doing is taking a full day off.

Lydia has an especially hard time with this because her work is truly bringing home the burritos. On most days, including weekends, she awakens to find student papers in her queue and a bunch of newsgroup messages to sift through from her online classes. Then the phone starts to ring around nine AM as students call on various questions and problems. Later in the day, our high-speed microwave Internet connection starts to act flakey, and until recently, the antenna kept being blown out of focus by strong winds. Now the mounting hardware is a lot stronger, but you get the picture. Lydia works her butt off seven days a week to keep us afloat.

So I try to treat her very nicely. While writing the now published book, I did receive some advanced royalties in three two-thousand dollar chunks. That helped me to feel I had at least a little income. But now that the book is published, royalties depend on sales, and sales have been slow due to the recession. The book itself has received a couple of good reviews, so I am confident that the market I targeted will come around once the economy revives.

Which will be when? Nobody knows.

I can just imagine what it is like for a lot of families and singles these days. I've heard it on talk radio during a program with a sympathetic guest. A woman called in sounding like one of the character's from *It's A Wonderful Life*, "But my husband hasn't worked for over a year, and I've got *bills to pay!*" Another man called in to report that he had tried to seek work of any kind, even if it pays half of what he earned before, and the markets for those kinds of jobs were as tight as everything else. Then another woman came on the air with a snotty voice. She was still employed and couldn't understand all these lazy people who can't find work. Her idea was for everyone to keep on calling employers every day, be persistent, and somehow get a job through the annoyance tactic. Well, that left the sympathetic guest a little speechless, dumbfounded by the ignorance this last woman displayed.

So what happens when unemployment runs out, your bills

lay around unpaid, and your job hunting efforts stall? Well, you can try an MLM (Multi-Level Marketing) outfit, which I did, and end up spending a lot more than you earn. Or you can try selling stuff on eBay, which I did, and find out that every Tom, Dick, and Mary has the same idea and can get the stuff at much lower wholesale prices than you can. Or you can just start selling off your assets, if you can find a buyer. I did this, too, with a guitar and a few other items of relatively high value that attracted eBay interest.

When my brother Rolph's family hit hard times in the 1980s, he joined up with an MLM. This one was a scam. After raising thirty thousand dollars by mortgaging the house, Rolph proceeded to sell the MLM to others. The product being touted was lawyer insurance. Did you know that lots of people get sued every year, and did you know that your legal fees to defend yourself could ruin you financially? Well now, here's the answer!

Rolph listened to all the tapes made by slick-talking motivational speakers, went to all the MLM meetings, bought himself an expensive silk suit, and failed miserably. Let's face it: Some people from Northern Minnesota might be good with sales among themselves, but nothing sounds stranger than one of my homeys trying to talk like a motivational speaker. Besides, everyone was out of work—how can you sell anything in an economic climate like that?

He soon had to borrow money from his wife's family to try to keep the failing MLM venture going. In the end, much was lost, but Rolph did find a way to pay back his wife's family. The point is to be careful with this MLM stuff. They seldom work out for the little people.

But ultimately, you need to find some way of making money. Hopefully, you have support from your spouse, family, friends—or hey, how about your church? Creating a flow of income when this situation is forced upon you is tough. Usually people who set out to create income save up money and seek out partners or investors to get the ball rolling. Lots of planning should be done to start a successful company or freelance career. Trying to pull this off on the fly might work, and it has worked for me—at least to a certain degree—but now the success depends almost entirely on the book buying habits of techies, and a lot of techies are out of work right now.

My first book has been published. The book idea had come to me a few years earlier, so that part was done. In addition, creating the outline and first three chapters, required by contract, went along smoothly because I had written them in my head already. It was just a matter of doing the research to verify and expand details, and then doing the word smithing. Coming up with the idea for this book took quite a bit longer, although I knew that the second book would be something about unemployment.

When we are reduced to scraping for a living, we need to try lots of different things before something starts to gel. Some of us are keeping our noses above water, if not our heads, yet there must be thousands of folks who haven't been able to find some other way of making an income. The news seems to be only reporting that hundreds of thousands have been laid off, millions if you go back to around 2000, but not much about what has been happening after layoff. We can probably guess that hundreds of thousands of people are scraping for a living any way we can. But that's not much consolation, just knowing that a lot of other folks are struggling as we are.

How many families have broken up? How many people have had to relocate, on their own credit cards, to some new place where the kids have to start a new school and the family has to rebuild friend relationships? How many have had to live out of their vehicles, as was common during the rust belt bust of the 1980s? How many have gone homeless, reduced to begging? A trend today is to make begging illegal, thus taking away a person's last means of survival short of thievery.

We have been fortunate to have found alternative ways. The fears of losing the house, being turned out on the street, and shaking the Styrofoam cup for loose change has haunted me often. I don't think we have deserved this, and I don't think this is a good reflection on our boast of being the best economy in the world. Big holes in the system are now exposed, and good people are falling through them at disturbing rates.

~ *5* ~

I Want to Be Like Mark Twain

What does it take to declare bankruptcy? You need a lawyer. You need a lawyer who specializes in this because you need to strategize your timing for bankruptcy. For example, I have no health insurance. If I get a serious illness that results in high hospital bills, I will be able to include those hospital bills in my bankruptcy. If this happens after the bankruptcy, I will be liable for those bills. So, in a sick sort of way, this is my health insurance while unemployed. My lawyer has advised me not to complete the bankruptcy until I get health insurance, either through a job or through my freelance writing income.

This lawyer charged $250 dollars as a retainer. When creditors call, I simply tell them that I have retained a bankruptcy lawyer, give his name, telephone number, and sometimes his address—and most of the time, I never hear from the creditors again.

You may think that doing this at the outset of your unemployment period is a good idea. I don't know if it is. One creditor wanted some history of how I got to this place, and I told her that I'd exhausted my unemployment compensation, the extension to the unemployment compensation, and now my income had reduced to zero. She seemed to like this answer. I don't know; you need to discuss this with a lawyer, and it never hurts to do this. I wish I'd have talked to my lawyer early on. That would have saved me a lot of heartache and worry. He would have charged me just $25 dollars for the consultation.

Do avoid the el-cheapo lawyers. All they do is file the documents to the court. You are on your own from there. In this state (Colorado), you can declare bankruptcy once every six years. Making this decision is not trivial: You will be treated like dirt by some organizations and individuals over the six-year period; others will salivate at offering you high-interest loans tied into your house or some other collateral. Some employers will balk at hiring you with a bankruptcy in your history. So, don't approach this without professional help. You will probably need around $2,500 to $3,000 dollars to finish the bankruptcy. This needs to be carefully planned too.

Lydia is six years older than me, and I am fifty years old. We are actually at good ages to declare bankruptcy due to our retirement funds having shrunk over the past couple of years. Lydia lost about two-thirds of her retirement fund. I didn't have much to begin with and cashed it in when unemployment came. So, we are looking at the next six years or so as being intensive saving times for retirement. The credit restrictions, along with all the shocks that accompany bankruptcy, will help us to achieve enough savings to retire. However, we don't plan to retire—so once this slump is over, the next boom comes, and the subsequent bust, we'll be better positioned for survival. We just want to keep the house and survive. We have enough stuff to keep us in freelance work, online work, and have a little fun. It is unfortunate that we need to stiff creditors who contributed to our stuff, but we did not do anything to bring the economy down, and we did not design the unsecured credit situation. Everyone, including unsecured creditors, take their chances. In addition, we have done everything we can to avoid bankruptcy. We do not take this lightly and punish ourselves emotionally more than anyone else could.

One of the bizarre corporate behaviors that we've heard of is the practice of offering unsecured credit to those who have just finished bankruptcy. This credit is never cheap! However, the risk of getting stiffed is low because you can't use bankruptcy as an out for a number of years. In any case, we think this is just too absurd for words.

You may be thinking that we should have never used so much unsecured credit in the first place. You may be right; you may be wrong. Plastic has brought us through tough times before. We may have gone homeless otherwise. It all depends on how lucky you are during hard times and what responsibilities you have taken on, including the raising of children. Both Lydia and I have raised children. I did so with Laurel over our six years together, and Lydia has raised two of her own children—and helped put them through college. The use of unsecured credit during certain times is actually a smart thing to do when your career is on a growth path, as ours have been: You borrow money, inflation (even though low) goes on, and so you pay back the loan with dollars of lesser value. Meanwhile, the lender has to keep interest rates relatively high to compensate, but you can shift your balance to lower interest credit cards, and so competition for your balance helps out.

When we were doing our remodeling and making the house a home, we used some unsecured credit for miscellaneous goodies. We've also used it to build up our computer equipment to support our respective careers. When I look back, our only sin was to have too much confidence in an economy that was falsely represented by many of its most important corporations. We trusted that the new Information Age economy was based on solid fundamentals, as did most professional investment outfits.

The infamous dot-com companies went down, as anyone with half a brain could have seen coming. You can't just throw billions of venture capital at startups and expect some magic return on investment, especially when a lot of the ideas were either bogus to begin with or outright frauds. Yet, IBM, Sun Microsystems, HP, Microsoft and slew of other important high-tech companies survived the crash. Telecom companies may be in trouble, but the latent demand for bandwidth keeps on growing, at least so I think. IBM's Global Services has been building out computing infrastructure to offer what is called *utility computing*, or in simple terms, computing power rentals. If I need more horsepower, storage capacity, or backup and disaster recovery support, I just pay IBM or some other provider for what I want. The business model is very similar to the utility companies that provide us with electricity, natural gas, and water. The thing to keep in mind is that these services have to go through telecommunication links, and that means more demand for bandwidth.

I don't understand this economy. Why has investment dried up so much, so quickly, and for so long? We can point to the war in Iraq, to the ongoing exposure of corporate cooked books, to the nasty vortex of consumer confidence, or maybe even to conspiracy theories about lowering wage expectations, but this all still leaves me with doubt that I'll ever understand why this recession has gone on for so long. Why did I need to be forced into bankruptcy?

Yes, we did buy some luxury items on credit. I built up my musical instrument collection and prepared to perform musically by getting a portable PA system and a used 4-track tape recorder for creating demonstration tapes. I'm an acoustic guitarist. This is my hobby. It may become part of my future profession and future income—as a result, I'll probably get to keep the equipment after bankruptcy.

However, we took this debt on with a combined income of over $120,000 per year. We had a five-year plan to pay off all debt while saving for retirement. The layoff and the cut in

Lydia's pay has brought us down to a potential income of only $40,000 between us. We have lost $80,000 of income over the course of a single year.

We can barely squeak by on $40,000 if we just have the mortgage and living expenses to cover. One of our vehicles is paid for, a 1994 Saturn. A 1998 Jeep Cherokee Sport still has another 18 months of payments at $285 a pop. We may sell that vehicle to eliminate the monthly bill. We may even make a few thousand off the deal. I have a 1996 Suzuki KLR 650 motorcycle that's paid for, a nice canoe, a popular handgun, and a few other items that can be sold. I'll probably keep the motorcycle because of its low sale value and its high potential as a source of writing material. I can take motorcycle excursions and write about those experiences in several different ways.

Will the bankruptcy court demand that we liquidate any of these small assets? Probably not. Is the house in jeopardy? No, not enough equity. What about the Saturn? Nope, can't take your only mode of transportation. What about what's left of Lydia's retirement fund? No. You need a good bankruptcy lawyer to advise you on all these issues. If you decide to go this route, try not to be too hard on yourself. You are small potatoes. The white-collar crooks who took billions from trusting souls—these people should suffer. But will they? Do they even have a conscious? Eh, it was all just doing business to them, probably.

Isn't it hilarious that these formerly respected leaders in our country now may be required to attend business ethics training? I think that is very funny. I wonder if they ever feel like they are in the headlamps? I hope so. Otherwise, these are truly lost souls.

Our lawyer tells us that many people do very well after

bankruptcy. Perhaps the relief of burden opens new doors of opportunity; perhaps the loss of pride releases suppressed talents; perhaps the fear of another bankruptcy spurs greater emphasis on saving over spending. The lawyer isn't sure why this happens because he isn't a psychiatrist, but it does seem to happen regularly. I know how I feel: I don't want this to ever happen again, and the loss of pride definitely opens up new doors in my mind regarding how to make money. But then, I'm not a psychiatrist either. I'm just me, broke and scraping for a living, depending very much on Lydia for a roof over my head, food in my belly, and encouragement to keep on trying.

I have had days where movement ahead seems futile. Hiring has been so slow for so long! The technical book didn't seem to be making any money. The next book wasn't gelling. My music practice became an oppression, and nothing gave pleasure. Hope seemed as distant as a new job, or more distant—another published work. Fear worked its way into the pours of my body to collect around my brain like concrete, slowly setting into rock hardness that no new idea could penetrate, like an underground bunker designed to withstand nuclear attack. What can you do but wait for this feeling to pass? Maybe watching some old movie will help. Maybe reading some book, or maybe just some prayer to keep on moving, keep on believing in better times ahead. This is not the same as being caught in the headlamps. This is complete and total depression, the stuff that nearly killed me in the 1980s. Yes, I know this feeling, this old companion. Not an enemy and not an evil, this is something more, and I suspect it is a necessary part of the human condition. It helps if you can release in some manner, at some point along the way, perhaps a few tears over some sappy old movie.

The failure of my six-year relationship with Laurel led to my successful relationship with Lydia. Perhaps my failure in bankruptcy will lead to future success. One of my heroes, Mark Twain, pulled this off. He had to do bankruptcy too, and he rose above his feelings of failure later on. I shall do the same.

Some days I feel very confident that all will pull into place, and I might not have to carry through with the bankruptcy. How could this happen? Winning the state lottery would do it. Winning Powerball would do it even better. Maybe I have a rich relative somewhere who will leave me a fat inheritance. It's funny how these improbable strings dangle before your eyes like the silk filaments of dream webs.

Still, what if the first book takes off, resulting in an enormously fat royalty check? That could happen, but since so many techies are out of work and broke like me, my market has dried up considerably. Besides, the lawyer informs me that copyrights might be up for grabs if they look too good. I'm conflicted then about the success of my books. But if they are really successful, what the heck, can't I pay off my creditors and be done with the whole issue? Ah-hah! The only reason to do bankruptcy in the first place is to clear the way for retirement savings. That means if I make a mountain of money, I'll have retirement bagged, too! So the heck with conflict. I want to be highly successful and to be like Mark Twain.

~ *6* ~
Reflections on Layoff and Recovery

When I got notice that my contract at WorldCom was not going to be renewed, I was elated. Good! Business had slowed down and I was confident that some other organization would pick me up quickly. Other outfits were doing big, important things! I'd also have some time to look around for other opportunities, practice my music, and take a little break from the daily grind.

Among my first moves on the job hunt was initiating a *resume blast* on the Internet. A resume blast is a service that you can buy from certain Websites that sends your resume electronically to thousands of potential employers all over the country. That was a waste of money because those resumes sent all over the place generated nothing but a lot of automatic email replies, and oddly enough, many regular USPS cards and letters saying thanks for nothing.

Something that worked better was to subscribe to a Web service that sent me feeds from all kinds of job boards on a daily basis, filtered by my keywords. This resulted in one email per day that gave me twenty or so job leads. The job leads linked to the job sites, and from there I could email my resume or apply online to the job. I could also register at the Websites I linked to, giving my information and uploading my resume.

I even started out on a technique I had learned earlier in my career development: networking. The idea of networking has changed over the years to where a lot of people think it is getting together with other unemployed people to discover if someone has come across a job that you might fit into. That's not the kind of networking I'm talking about. If you explore the ideas in the book, *What Color Is Your Parachute*, you will discover that, although support groups are discussed, real networking involves seeking out a hiring manager through a network of professionals in your chosen field. But first you need to choose the field and know exactly what kinds of specific jobs you are qualified for, based on the skill matrix you've built.

But times would become progressively tougher for finding a job. Layoffs seemed to be coming weekly, and this flooded the market with techies looking for work. The competition became steadily stiffer. In addition, the people I tried to contact in the initial phase of networking were all tight-lipped. Something was going on. Why was everyone so secretive? Since it seemed that virtually nobody was hiring—or even talking—I decided to try some alternative ways of making money.

One of those efforts was to send out a query letter to several technical book publishers asking if they'd be interested in a book about storage management. Storage management involves the installation, configuration, and support of large computer disk arrays, automated tape libraries, and various other technologies designed to store and preserve massive amounts of data. One publisher, Apress, expressed interest by requesting a preliminary introduction for the book and a detailed outline.

I had been thinking of writing this book for some time because I had a lot of storage management experience in both the mainframe and midrange (Unix) worlds. The introduction came easily, as did the outline. Soon after Apress accepted this material, I had a contract to finish the prepublishing draft of the book by August of 2002.

Writing has always come easy to me. I suppose a person is born with this ability, but it does take a lot of training to write well, especially when using the English language. But here I was, fifty years old, highly experienced in large computing environments, five years of technical writing under my belt, and sitting on an almost-finished degree in English. Could I actually finish this book? Would it actually go to press? Was I becoming a real writer?

I remember one morning when I was up early, around four, and came down to the room I use for serious writing. It's on the ground level of our three-story house and has a nice view of some trees and a corner of Pikes Peak. I have a small table, bookshelves, built-in nook, futon couch, bathroom/shower, sink, coffee pot, and a side room where I have my guitars and can take a break to play music should the desire come. This is the perfect writer's area. I have privacy and inspiration—a short hop out the French doors to the small front deck, then a climb up a black metal circular staircase to an upper deck for magnificent mountain views. It is an idyllic setting that any writer would want. But then one early morning, I stared at my computer screen and could not write. My heart was full of dread: Can I actually pull this off? Am I good enough? What if they cancel the contract because I suck? These feelings kept me from writing for a solid week. Back in the headlamps, frozen solid, I needed something to break the spell.

There's a thing called *writer's block*, and that is tough enough. Writer's block involves losing the ability to string words together into some coherent whole. This was not writer's block; this was writer's defeat. I could still string words together, but I had lost faith in myself to be able to do a marketable, commercially acceptable piece of work. My sylvan, quiet writer's environment mocked me—you suck and you know it. Voices from my early adult years haunted me: Who do you think you are? You're nothing but low class like us. You have no talents! Get a dishwasher's job. College? Screw a bunch of college. Go get a job, you lazy professional student. Computers? There's no future in computers. Come on back to Northern Minnesota—the mines are hiring! Writer? Musician? You're dreaming, Ray. You suck and you know it.

That was the worst week of my life (so far). Anger transformed to depression, which moved into torpid angst. I decided that another project was needed to get my mind off this track, out of those headlamps, and onto a completely different path. I began serious guitar study with the intent of building enough repertoire for full-length gigs. Would this work? Might not the torturing voices hit me on music too?

My morning schedule changed from writing first thing to music first thing. I spent two to three hours every morning working on new and old repertoire. After just a few days, I was back to writing on the book in the late morning and all afternoon. My production on both the music and writing zoomed along.

Probably every writer has to get through that phase of self-doubt. I would not wish this experience on anyone, but if you want to be a writer, maybe this is a rite of passage. Come to think of it, I'll bet every profession has some kind of rite like this. It's just that when you are on your own, whether typing on a keyboard for publication or performing music for money, the passage rites come squarely onto your own self-image. Your tender little ego is at stake.

Maybe that's why musicians get these overly inflated egos—it's a defense against admitting that you suck. Or maybe it is some sort of natural brain drug that kicks in when you actually succeed at something. Well, with musicians this could be artificial brain drugs. This isn't a good example. Let me go back to writers.

Do writers get overly inflated egos? I'm trying to think of a writer like this, and I'm drawing a blank. I don't think so. I think writers have egos that get toughened over time, just like my fingertips grow thick calluses the more I play guitar. After that first book is published, you have physical proof of your abilities. You also know that the first book is far from perfect. The next one will be better. Rereading my first book shows me that I could have done this or that differently. I can see where more could have been added here and there, and I cringe at the few typographical or grammatical errors in the finished product. Granted, other good writers have edited my initial submissions and ending up with some errors in a finished product is bound to happen, but you still see those glaring errata. However we writers decide to disturb our natural states of Nirvana with nagging realities, the fact of the matter is that writing has never come so easily to me after publishing the first book. My ego is well encased in hard keratin like the feet of deer are protected by hooves. How can ego over inflate when armored like this? I know I am a good writer; I am a commercially published writer—and here, between the covers of the first book, is the undeniable proof.

The way Apress handles publishing is interesting. All of my initial submissions were composed with Microsoft Word and sent to the publisher as email attachments. An editor would markup the text with corrections and give some feedback on what might be confusing or poorly composed prose, and then send back the Word file as another email attachment. Once all the chapters had gone through this process, Apress converted the Word files to electronic galley sheets in the Adobe Acrobat format. These were emailed to me for final review.

My book used a lot of graphics to illustrate how computer storage worked, how it could be configured, and various other ideas. I started using a high-end graphics package to create these illustrations, but that was just too clumsy for what I was doing. Microsoft Paint, a very simple graphics program that comes free with Microsoft operating systems, became my preferred tool. The graphic artist assigned to my project could have converted directly from Paint to her high-end graphics program, but I had deleted all my Paint files after doing screen captures of them. My assumption was that the screen captures would be the best to use for publishing because Apress had provided me the program (SnagIt) for free. The lesson here is to keep all your files until the book has actually been published and rests in your proud hands. However, I was lucky to have a talented, creative artist who discovered a way to convert the screen captures to her desired format.

This book was created and produced entirely by electronic means. No physical galley sheets had to be USPS-mailed or faxed to me for review. I did not have to USPS-mail or fax them back. This resulting efficiencies of using electronic communication for book creation resulted in a publish date of October, 2002 for *Unix Storage Management* by Ray A. Kampa and Lydia V. Bell.

Well, okay, I admit to having just a little bit of ego inflation over this accomplishment. Becoming a published writer is every English major's dream, whether we admit to it or not.

One of the surprising outcomes of writing this book has been advice from contract agents (those people who can find me a technical job) to not mention the book on my resume. Lydia thinks it is because this really sets us apart from the competition, and not in a positive way. Hiring managers are probably intimidated by published authors! No, that can't be. These are educated people! How can they carry such a prejudice? But the farther we go along this path, the more this becomes apparent. We intimidate people just for being who we are. So does this mean we are contacting the wrong people? Are we at a different level now, and just what are these levels? How many are there? Where the hell did they come from?

There's another side to this too. I had an interview for a technical position not long ago, and the team lead guy escorted me out afterwards. He wanted to know how I ever got this book deal. He was curious, interested, and maybe had a book idea of his own. I gave him the two-minute summary of query letter, introduction/outline composition, first three chapters, contract, and the electronic communications publishing technique. I don't know, but maybe this has inspired a future writer of commercially accepted technical books.

I have decided to leave my book on my resume, and to hell with those who find it intimidating. I don't want to work for that type of person anyway.

Getting back to the first few months of layoff, I was granted an extra week with Ciber, the contracting outfit that paid my salary but stationed me in WorldCom. I have to hand it to Ciber's management—they did all they could to find me another position. My extra week became a full work-from-home deal where I researched the Internet for network performance information and answers to related questions. This helped me to retain the self-assuredness that had grown over a long, successful career in computers.

This feeling—having great optimism and a bounce in my step, and perhaps even a little swagger—was not to last for long. The first crack that opened was my experiences with filing for unemployment compensation. I negotiated the bureaucracy to the point of being in the county unemployment office for my appointment, and there I sat down among other unemployed folks.

Across from me was a young mother with her infant baby. She looked at me with sad doe eyes, a woman accustomed to struggling day-to-day. Empty chairs flanked her. In the same row sat a young man, shaven head, pierced face and wearing work clothes from WalMart. He seemed alienated and distant, lost in his own thoughts and feelings. Hispanic faces seemed the majority on the other side of the room, patiently awaiting their turns in the system.

An older man, perhaps my age (it becomes harder to tell as you age), dressed in a business suit and holding a leather briefcase, hung his head and peered at the tiled floor. This seemed to be the side of the room for old farts. A rotund older woman entered, signed up, and sat near me. With twinkling eyes, she wished me a good morning. I struck up a conversation:

"Good morning to you! How goes the job hunt?" I asked.

"Oh, I'm just starting. I was managing a gas station, but they bumped me for a younger thing. You know how it goes," she answered, giving a little wink.

"Yeah, but that still sucks. So you don't have any bad feelings about that?"

"Why should I? It's just the way things are. You get older and you get pushed aside. But, yes, maybe I do feel resentment. I was a good manager. Everyone liked me, even when I had to use discipline, but after raising seven kids, you learn how to work with the teens and twenties," she replied, her brightness diminishing.

She folded her hands in her lap. I thought she might be praying, and so kept silent for a while. Then, with a nod, she turned her face, now with less twinkle, to mine. "Why are you here? Were you caught in all those high tech layoffs?" she asked, smiling kindly.

I told her the brief version of my story. She asked if I thought age had anything to do with the decision, and I answered that it probably didn't. The demand for my work had gone down and, since I was a contractor, I was first to the chopping block. She looked down again briefly, and then:

"It must be nice to know that it wasn't your age and appearance that swayed the decision."

That just floored me. How unjust! But what was she to do? Hiring a lawyer to bring suit probably wasn't her nature, even if she had the money. I could feel her heavy reliance on her faith to get her through this hard time and hoped that her faith was not misplaced. If there is a God and a savior Jesus Christ, then by gosh, this woman deserved the comfort and strength that having faith in these deities promise. So I silently asked God and Jesus to please stay true to her, along with any other spirit that would listen and help.

Our names were called for orientation and meetings with our respective counselors. We wished each other good fortune and rapid success.

My counselor was a nice young woman who genuinely wanted to help, but she had never worked with techies much. She didn't understand what we did for a living. She was accustomed to working with truck drivers, welders, mechanics, cooks, waitresses, landscapers, janitors, bank tellers, and all sorts of people who do recognizable work in our world. All the acronyms and mysterious language on my resume was gibberish to her, so I tried to explain in normal English that I kept big computing systems going, using her desktop computer and LAN as a reference. She seemed to get a few glimmers of insight, but in the end she told me that I'd probably do a better job of sorting through their job openings than she could.

While driving up the pass from Colorado Springs, I thought

a lot about the woman who prayed. Was she to hold her faith or become bitterly resentful toward deities who reneged on their promises? I tended to think that her faith had been exercised plenty of times while raising her children, and so she is accustomed to disappointment in prayers not being answered, or the answer being "no." Nevertheless, I asked all the deities I could think of to help her out. I am an equal opportunity praying person.

It took several weeks for my panic to develop. After sending out hundreds of resumes and being rebuked at networking, my mind extrapolated what might happen into the future. Well, we could lose everything! Become homeless! Beg for a living!

Or not. Lydia did much to keep my head level during that time of shedding professional pride. She bolstered me by praising my writing abilities and the possibilities that a whole new career was opening up for me. I thanked the deities for her presence, love, and support.

Another bad emotion that I had to deal with was the feeling of being useless. We do take a great deal of pride in our work, generally speaking, and when each day becomes a challenge to carry out, that nasty voice screaming, "Loser! Bum! Deadbeat!" can grow strong. I suppose a Christian would call that the voice of the Devil, but it sounds so darn familiar when it haunts my consciousness. Was that Rolph? Rick? My father or mother? Somebody ranting away on talk radio? Hey, it could be old Scratch himself imitating the sound of familiar voices.

I think the Christian advice to pray the voices away can help, as can getting busy on what needs to be done. Back when I was a teenager, I had suicidal urges and realized that I was feeling useless in the world. The way out of that back then was to set some goals and work towards them. My young goals were simple: get the car running, work on the motorcycle, date around with girls, have some fun with my friends, and drive about Northern Minnesota with loud rock music coming from my eight-track stereo linked to eight speakers. It was loud!

Unemployment must then regress us back to feeling like useless teens in the world. Our adult pride has been taken away, and now we must beg for employment—any employment— from people who are already employed, and who may not understand the enormous pressures we job seekers are under.

And so, I went from a high degree of self-confidence to rock bottom, and stayed there for months. I suspect this is a normal regression, but the good news is that being on rock bottom leaves only one way to proceed—upward. However, I experienced several layers of rock bottom, as if I was falling off a stepped mesa. Bam! Hit bottom with the bad job market. Wham! Another bottom of collecting unemployment compensation. Whump! Unemployment compensation exhausted. Slam! Retain a bankruptcy lawyer.

Then, while on each level of rock bottom, I'd be punching myself in the guts over my inability to write, to publish, to play guitar, or to even enjoy a nice day in the mountains. Meanwhile, nobody was being nasty to me, or at least most people were not. One was, and that was very tough to take. We are so vulnerable, the unemployed.

We can, and we must, use everything at our disposal to survive. I really do think praying helps, even though I'm not Christian. Keeping busy helps, even if it involves a hobby that has nothing to do with career or making a living. Appreciating the people who love us helps, and these relationships must be maintained above all else. We, the unemployed, face serious challenges each and every day as we fall to rock bottom and struggle to rise again. The terms hope, faith, and love mean more to us now than, possibly and probably (in my mind), any other times in our lives.

Perhaps this is a good thing. Perhaps our pride needed to fall, and now needs to grow into something more important. I hope and have faith that real compassion comes of all this, along with the ability to share in another's prayers, however we may think of that.

~ 7 ~

Talking Economy Blues

Yesterday, Sunday the 29th of January, 2002, we were both depressed. Depression is nothing new to us, and it certainly isn't anything uncommon since the layoff, but sometimes your mind heads outward some months ahead, and the notion of homelessness creeps in. Homelessness. Losing the house, bankruptcy for both of us, shunned from society, outcasts in our fifties. This isn't good for anybody: not the bankruptcy part, not the homeless part, and not the depression part.

Our nation is supposed to be the best on earth. We know it is a lot better than nations where starvation and warring factions are common, but if you don't plan for the ore train's headlamps, or you don't plan well enough, you can become destitute very quickly. Something is wrong with a system that encourages huge riches while pushing our means to plan for the future down. Most people will never attain the billions of dollars that the nation's leaders, and by this I mean the real leaders—business people, grasp onto and hold jealously close. Now I don't mean to say that all business people with billions of dollars are inherently evil. No. All of us are the same in this respect. Greed begets greed. That is just basic human nature. What I mean to say is that once you become rich, it is just natural to become tempted into the corruption of heart and soul. Few people can resist this basic grasping—this fundamental need to keep and grow wealth.

Other older cultures, as those in Europe, have come to grips with the basic nature of humankind and have created more socialistic conditions where wealth simply can't pool into a small percentage of the population. We in the United States generally snort at this situation. Socialism, isn't that the same as communism? Didn't we fight the Cold War against communism, and didn't we contain it in Vietnam? Well, we at least slowed it down for a time.

Socialism, doesn't that system kill the human spirit? Doesn't the United States come up with all the best inventions? Aren't Europeans clamoring at our doors to immigrate into the United States, emigrate out of Europe? What's so great about Europe?

I don't know, but I do know this: Having your basic needs of food, water, air, clothing, shelter—and dare I add a feeling of self-worth—provided by the society in which you live is the only reason societies were founded in the first place. We in the United States have forgotten that and choose to believe that society exists primarily to give us all a shot at getting rich. Most of us won't get rich. Some of us won't even get to the middle class. Too many of us live like bums.

Well, a lot of those bums live like that because they want to, so the rationalization goes. No, not a lot. Some. Most would rather have a decent job with a decent income, live in decent conditions, and have some modest hope for the future.

Our society is a guilty one. We need a lot of churches to go to and pray for forgiveness for our callousness. The most popular god has taken on the sins of the world so we don't have to. Our think tanks work hard and long to justify what we do to each other and our environments. The rich fund and promote radio talk shows, newspapers, magazines, books, Web sites, and television programs to make a little bit of profit and a lot of propaganda. The propaganda is that socialism is evil. We don't want socialism.

All right, so we don't want socialism. Maybe we want

something better than socialism. If we are the best educated and most creative of societies, then we ought to be able to come up with a better scheme.

One of our biggest problems is the business cycle. Nobody really likes this cycle. You're up one year, in the ditch the next. Too many of us just accept it as a given and even speculate when things will go one way or another. Some people become rich betting that the business cycle will head downwards, a situation that usually shocks people who are just learning about investing. We tend to think that capitalism is designed to build successful companies, not failures. Ah well, this is just one of many contradictions in capitalism. Rewarding corporate officers for doing their jobs poorly is another—hiring and promoting on the basis of family connections is another. Capitalism has a lot of problems. It can't be the best system possible.

What would be a better system? I'm not sure, but we won't find one until we look. Simply accepting capitalism as the best defeats any attempt at finding something better. Dismissing thoughts along these lines as being "unrealistic," "idealistic," and "utopian" jabbering from hopeless dreamers also defeats any attempt at improvement, and that happens to be the agenda for a lot of very rich people. Maintenance of power is at the core of this train of thought, at least from what I've seen.

The capitalistic system imploded in the 1930s. This resulted in more socialism in the United States in the forms of job programs, relief programs, strong unions, higher taxes, bigger military, and what is called "pork" for the states, or rather, a form of job program that involves specific projects. None of this generates revenue. All of it costs tax money collected from organizations and individuals who do generate revenue.

Since the 1930s, we have fought many wars. Our military

grew and grew into a major tax-subsidized employer. Military contractors supply the hardware and software of war; our families provide the "wetware," that is, the human soldiers. Since 9/11, our annual military budget has grown past the $350 billion it had been. Right now, the price tag for having the biggest military and the being the highest military spender in the world approaches the $400 billion mark, or $400,000 million. Divide this number by our present population count (around 260 million), and we spend $1,538 to defend one United States citizen each and every year.

We are supposed to be spending this money to defend the citizens of the United States. In actuality, a good portion of this expenditure goes toward situations that have nothing to do with defending United States citizens. Some of this money finds its way to clever business people who buy military surplus for small dollars and then resell the surplus back to the military for big dollars. Some of the money is used for frivolous luxuries that a handful of military personnel enjoy, and some of it is simply wasted to support obsolete weapons programs or straight-up pork weapons programs.

To be fair, a large portion of our federal budget goes towards the Medicare, Medicaid, and Social Security programs—all a part of a scheme often referred to as socialistic. Also, to be more fair, different groups interpret the federal budget in different ways in order to press their particular political agendas. The federal government itself formats the budget numbers to deemphasize military spending and to emphasize social spending, or so some critics have contended.

This all gives me a headache. Our household budget is simple because we don't make nearly what we made before the layoff, and the prospects for regaining even half of that income back look discouraging. Depression enters our lives regularly as we cut back, sell off, and seriously consider what we will do if we lose the house.

What could possibly be a better system than we have now? Well, we could stop pretending that we are not a socialistic country and just embrace the system as a whole. We could do away with pork that masks the reality of a scattered and inefficient job program. We could do away with Medicaid and Medicare, along with our very inefficient way of giving healthcare to the poor (including the unemployed), and fund a true national healthcare system. We could also overhaul our military structures for efficiency, and although some movement has been made in this direction, perhaps we ought to make it a national goal.

Alternatively, we could abandon socialism altogether. We could eliminate all pork job programs, drop Social Security, throw out Medicare and Medicaid, reduce taxes considerably, and hope that free market capitalism can somehow keep everyone employed at decent wages with decent benefits.

I don't see either way as being plausible. The inertia that has developed in our country over the decades and centuries is enormous. However, this inertia hasn't resulted in an unmovable object that needs an irresistible force to move it about, as would be the case with a dictatorship and the resulting revolution or regime change through invasion. Change has been coming, but slowly.

For example, the idea of using hydrogen as an alternative fuel to petroleum products, natural gas, and possibly coal has come into the mainstream debate. If you want to know more about this idea, try doing an Internet search on "hydrogen economy," or search your local library's card catalog on the same keywords.

I come from the political side that thinks government and

private industry have and still can work together to bring about massive and beneficial change to our society. For example, the REA (Rural Electrification Administration) brought electricity to small towns, farms, and ranches. This in turn raised the demand for electric lights and appliances. The Interstate Highway System brought us a high-speed limited access highway network that boosted the trucking industry, tourism, and the roadside service industry, not to mention the oil industry. NASA got us into space and on the moon while delivering Velcro and Teflon, among many other technical advances.

When I distribute my published book via the USPS, I can use the media rate, which comes to about $1.85 per book for shipment within the United States and its territories. Try to get that rate from FedEx or UPS.

My point is that government programs are not inherently doomed to failure, no matter what the conservative propagandists wish us to think.

Now, what is going to get this economy off its back? Will it be tax cuts targeted to the rich or some form of job program that promotes hiring back laid off employees? What about a special training program for displaced people who need to update skills? We have a war on terrorism and drugs, why not a war on unemployment?

Ah, here's a sticky situation. Private enterprise likes a large pool of unemployed labor. This keeps the cost of labor down while encouraging the cutting back of benefits. Hey, it's just business, right? Right. But this business is not in society's best interests. It literally enforces a percentage of the population into poverty and homelessness. In other words, capitalism is, at its fundamental core, flawed. It is flawed because those of us who want to work cannot always find work, and when the business cycle tanks, and stays tanked over a period of not months but years, this puts honest, hard-working, family folks into jeopardy of intense poverty and even homelessness. I am sorry, but this is not evidence of a successful system.

Back when I was in college, I took a course in macro economics. The professor liked to egg me on because he thought I was against capitalism and for socialism, this due to the long length of my thick hair and my ratty student clothes. Naw, I was just poor and didn't like haircuts. Through this egging on, it came up that I was from a Northern Minnesota mining family, and this gave the professor even more stimulus to try to yank my chain.

"So, Kampa," he'd say while posturing in his three-piece business suit, "What do you think of these trees being planted on the mall? Is that ecologically sound?"

I didn't think so. You let trees plant themselves in a healthy ecology, and the minute you start gardening them, you've taken on the responsibilities that nature already carries out. No, the ecological problem is development itself. Building the mall screwed up this little piece of the ecology. But what does that have to do with macro economics?

The professor gave me an intense look. "Because, Kampa, the development of natural resources is necessary in any economic system. Land is a natural resource, and so it must be developed."

"Oh?" I countered, "all right, let's say the entire earth becomes developed. We now manage everything in the ecosphere. Will that stop the hearty seedling from poking its head arrogantly through the concrete and blacktop we've laid, and make itself manifest despite our best efforts to manage something much greater than our collective selves? I've seen this happen, professor, as I walked along an old, abandoned highway while hunting grouse near my hometown. We may think we control our environment, but that will always turn out to be an illusion. Ma Nature will not be put down by our puny efforts to keep a mall treed or tree-free."

The professor kinda liked my argument, so he moved on to unemployment.

"I read where your brothers are thinking of striking the mining companies up north. What do you think about that?"

He held the lapels of his suit as he laid that low blow of family loyalty on me. I rolled with the punch and talked about how a healthy capitalistic economy needs to tolerate a four to five percent unemployment rate. I gave my rebuttal:

"The strike isn't about the unemployment rate as much as other business practices of the company, such as contracting nonunion labor even though plenty of union labor is available. However, professor, I question the validity of the premise that a four to five percent unemployment rate is tolerable for those who are unemployed. As one of my brothers says, 'A recession is when others are unemployed; a depression is when you are unemployed.'"

The professor liked that answer too, but I just couldn't squeeze better than a B grade from him. Still, I remember him fondly and wish the best for him now. If nothing else, we entertained each other.

The point is that unemployment rates mask the reality of numbers. When we talked about a percentage point of unemployment in 1973, this translated to a number of individuals that was vastly smaller than a percentage point of unemployment represents today. As a result, some economists are thinking that a 2-3% rate is today's tolerable level of unemployment. And still I ask, tolerable for whom? Certainly not the unemployed.

Well, I hope this overly long business contraction turns out for the better. I hope the overly idealistic notions of free markets takes it in the chops as people hit rock bottom not once, but multiple times on the way to the street. I hope the rich realize that something more bold than tax cuts has to be done, and I am afraid that summertime riots in big cities may be coming our way to bring the message straight on home.

I think that may be coming, although the only good result would be an awakening of all of America to the realities people are facing these days. I sure don't want riots to break out, and I didn't want them to break out in the 1960s and 70s either, but they did. I can see it coming and can't do anything to stop it other than write about what we might consider doing to make things better for everyone.

We need to drop this cult of greed and stop worshipping money. How we do this is beyond my ken, but I think the humility many of us have learned, or relearned, has helped. A buck means a lot more to me now than when I was employed.

We need to think more about society as a whole rather than maintaining blind loyalty to ideologies, teams, factions, and parties. We need to think outside these boxes within boxes within even more boxes to come up with creative solutions to our problems, such as moving from a carbon-based energy infrastructure to a hydrogen-based reality. We need to keep everyone who wants to work working, while keeping the entrepreneurial spirit alive for those with the visions, energies, resources, talents, and drives to build what can be from where we stand now.

We need to stop mourning what once was and accept the past as being the history it is. We need to work with what we've got to build better futures for ourselves, our children, and the generations to come. Mourning, mercifully, is a transient state of mind.

We need to admit to the realities of the world, join with brilliant minds of all nations, and work toward common peace and security. Granted, the neo-conservatives have their visions of what this might entail, and I invite you to search the Internet for more information on what the neo-conservative agenda is. To me, it entails world dominance but in a more digestible form than it has been presented in the past. It does, however, still head toward dominance.

And, finally, we must survive. To let our lower-level urges of hatred and revenge cloud our thinking as we move onward into this century and as domestic and world politics shift within cyclone winds of change, we need courage.

Hey, that came off pretty well! Maybe I can get a job in politics?

An old blues tune comes to mind:

Crying won't help you. Praying might do you some good, from "When The Levee Breaks," for those of you with interest.

~ *8* ~
A New Year, Still Unemployed

Today is January 1, 2003. A new year has begun, and to bring this year in with a hopeful note, snow falls outside the French doors we use as the main entrance to our little place in the Rocky Mountains across from Pikes Peak. Louise Armstrong toots his trumpet on the PBS radio station transmitted from the liberal arts school in Colorado Springs, the Colorado College. I smoke cheap cigarettes purchased online from an Indian reservation out east, drink bargain coffee lightened with bulk-purchased powdered coffee creamer. Ella Fitzgerald joins Louise with her silky voice as the tune drifts into its soft ending, and another classic jazz piece comes across the airwaves. This one is upbeat—a big band dance tune.

Today marks the end of a period that always depresses Lydia. We are so tightly attuned to each other's emotions that the depression pulls me down too, although the holiday season has never been a very good one for me either. Actually, that's not quite right. We both remember happier times as young children before we became aware of the pain to be found in this world. A PBS news report mentioned the death of Hank Williams on this day so many years ago. His last record had been released on this day: *I'll Never Get Out Of This World Alive*.

Lydia's stepfather shot himself on Christmas day while she was around eleven years old. Her older sister died from a brain aneurism on Christmas day in 1991, just when Lydia and I were beginning our relationship. I was visiting her at the time. She lived in Lakewood, Colorado, which is an old suburb of

Denver. I remember clearly her face as she came into the bedroom, crying, with the sad news. A few years later, her mother died near the Christmas holidays. This time of year has become one of dread and depression for her.

But now, as the snow gently accents the trees and hills with white frostings, as it brings the purity of a year just a few hours old, and as the memories of people who have passed on, people whom I have loved—some who may have done me wrong—as these memories drift in and out, swirling like the snow outside, I feel bright and hopeful. We will keep this beautiful place; we will find ways to make more money and survive. We are creative, talented people. We have been down before and always came back up. Unemployment, bankruptcy, and starting over again aren't so bad. We have made it to the new year and nobody we know has died.

A couple of jobs that I might fit into opened up in Colorado Springs yesterday. One is very low paid and involves just monitoring system backups. The other is a genuine Unix systems administration job that probably pays twice as much. I hope I get that one, but I am willing to work for the lower wage too.

Pride doesn't go far for paying the mortgage, although there are some things I won't do out of my sense of honor. I won't write college papers for online paper mills, for example. I'd rather work in fast food for minimum wage than help to further dilute the meaning of a college education. Students must write their own papers because this is a big part of the education process. I will review and edit their English, but that's it. The review process itself is designed to encourage the students to become better writers. I like that.

The small bit of larceny I've taken on is that the papers are actually assigned to Lydia to review. She has the college degrees; I don't. I don't even have a bachelor's degree. But I can write; I have a commercially published book; I have almost four years toward a bachelor's degree, and I am a darn good editor who believes strongly in the education process, whether this is acknowledged through a degree or not.

I am also writing the lectures for her online classes. We add a copyright notice at the bottom that attributes the writing to me. Our rationalization is that Lydia communicates directly with her students through newsgroup posts, telephone calls, and when required, face-to-face meetings. She does the instruction, and I do the writing/editing. Is it wrong that I don't have a college degree when I have the ability to do these tasks for Lydia? The University may someday punish us for this stretching of the rules. Maybe we'll be featured on the six o'clock news as being criminals in the university system. Or maybe the anal retentiveness of the university system will change to where professionals, no matter if degreed or not, can teach their subjects of mastery.

Perhaps when our income improves, I will return to Mankato State University and finish my degree. I owe them about 16 credits, some in English and the others in speech. I've already researched this and contacted the chair of the English department to verify what needs to be done. It is about a semester's worth of effort.

But why didn't I finish my degree back in 1975? Well, I had run out of money for one thing. During my last quarter (Mankato was on a quarter system back then), I was working full time as an automotive parts guy and still pulled a perfect 4.0 average using the independent study method of research and writing. I felt that I had learned all that I needed to learn to continue through life as a lifelong student of everything. Another reason I dropped out was that I felt the real world held more adventure for me in that I could prove just how far you can go without a sheepskin. Bill Gates of Microsoft has shown this as well. You can go a long ways without college degrees, but Bill sure went a lot farther than I did, if you consider money as the metric. I'll go head-to-head with him if other metrics are considered, such as richness of true feelings. I don't think Bill Gates really has much of a soul. But then, I don't really know the guy either—just his public persona, and that is always false.

Most people should get their college degrees, so I believe. It takes some sort of bug up the rear for people like me to build a career without a degree. I also must confess that during the economic meltdown of the 1980s in Colorado, I fudged on my resume. I claimed to have had a bachelor's degree in English. This might have helped me to land a job with Federal Express in Memphis, Tennessee, but I doubt it. Later, because I just left the myth in place, I lost a job with a government contractor due to the fudging. Since then I have just claimed the truth: about 4 years of college education, English major, 3.4 GPA.

What causes people to fudge their resumes? I suppose they do this for the same reason I did it, because they feel desperate to get a job. I also suppose employers expect a certain amount of fudging to be going on, and that the interview process is designed in part to determine what might and what might not have been fudged.

Now that I have so many years in the industry, I've actually removed a good portion of my experience on the current resume. My mainframe systems programmer years are all lumped together into a short blurb with four bulleted points. This represents fourteen years of my life!

But that doesn't count to a lot of employers. It may even be intimidating to those hiring managers who may have only five or six years of experience in the computing field. Some employers may think that as soon as something better comes up, I will be gone. What's wrong with that? Aren't we working within a free-market employment situation? These employers seem not to think twice about laying off loyal employees. Why do they expect one-way loyalty? Loyalty has never worked this way and it never will—unless the situation is something like a dictatorship. Employers who have no local competition for employees often fall into the dictatorial illusion.

I wish there was more mutual loyalty between employers and their employees. I wish that the relationship was stronger. I wish corporate officers behaved in more responsible ways. I wish we had a better system. These are my wishes for the new year, besides the wish to again be employed in a good job with good pay and the potential for growth within my chosen career.

The snow still falls. Once it stops, I will be shoveling and snow-blowing. The sun will come out and do its magic on the driveway by clearing it with bright, warm, yellow light streaming down from deep blue skies. Steam will rise from the blacktop. Water will flow toward streams, rivers, and reservoirs. Seeds buried by industrious squirrels in the blackened soils at the edge of the Hayman wildfire area will awaken slightly to take a mid-winter sip.

Our own creative seeds are stirring after this difficult season, too. Hopefully the work through the University will continue until something else comes up. Perhaps this is my year to start making money through my music. This book will be completed, that's for certain. I believe an honest book about what it is like to be seeking employment when little employment is to be found is a necessary thing.

One thing I've noticed about the career planning and job hunting books I've used along the way is that the authors don't seem to know much about being unemployed. They tend to counsel for a situation in which they have little direct experience, much like a celibate priest counseling a married couple on sexual difficulties. Yes, yes, the theory sounds good and flows logically, but in the real world, anything can and does happen. However, the whole situation is really quite simple. You want a job. A job needs to be available. The hiring manager must want you. When these three things come together, an offer for employment usually follows.

Yet the emotions and intellectual tricks used in this process complicate what ought to be a simple process. I often find myself being interviewed by two or more people at once. This immediately brings the complexity of group dynamics into play. If one of these interviewers doesn't like you, the job is probably lost. How can you make everyone like you? I wish I knew.

I am adding this part of the chapter after having had my interview for the low-paying backup monitoring position. I didn't get the job, although the interview seemed to go well and the hiring manager seemed to want me, or at least respected my age and experience. The lead guy seemed to like me. One other person in the interview seemed to be displeased that I lacked a degree. She had a master's degree in something and a bachelor's degree in English. I was tempted to ask what she has published, but then I thought that maybe this would anger her more. People who major in English have a dream to one day become published authors. Few actually realize this dream and become, instead, bored copy writers, technical writers, editors, journalists, and so on. The job was offered to someone who has experience with the particular flavor of software this company was using for backups—that was the reason given for passing me by. Since this is a fairly weak reason, I can speculate that other issues were at the base of this decision.

Here's where you can get into big trouble with yourself. Why wasn't I chosen? What is wrong with me? Feelings of rejection and lack of worth creep in. I started down that path for a brief period of time until a realization came to me: I did not want that job, even though I put up an effort to seem interested. I am sorry, monitoring backups, even world-wide backups, is just too narrow for me. And so, it didn't matter who wanted me in that position—I did not want it. All three elements: available job, wanting the job, and being wanted for the job—must be in place before an offer comes.

What makes hiring managers and influential people in the hiring decision like you? I doubt this can be faked. I doubt anybody can act his or her way into making people respond with feelings that surround the idea of "liking." No salesperson can force you to like anything; all that can be done is gentle persuasion.

People tend to like other people who remind them of someone they have liked before. They tend to like people who are interested in the same things as themselves. They may like you simply because of the general feeling about you, or as the psychics call it, your aura. Every job offer I have received came from someone who decided to like me. The thing is that not everyone is going to like you. That's just the way things go in life. Some people will actually dislike you a lot, and you may be subjected to some psychological torture in these situations.

Early on in my career (before learning about career development), back when I was seeking some job—any kind of job—near Minneapolis, I interviewed with a telecommunications equipment manufacturing company. Part of this process was a math test. The hiring manager liked me, and I did quite well on the math test, which consisted of a timed series of simple addition, multiplication, and division problems. The job involved computer operations. Everything was going smoothly until the mandatory meeting with the vice president of computer operations came up. That guy hated my guts. Why? I don't know, but he sure was cold with me, and there was nothing I could do or say to change his mind. Did I threaten him somehow? Was I too self-assured? Perhaps he didn't like English majors who could also do math. Maybe I was too smart to be a computer operator. That must have been it!

You can be too smart, too competent, too honest, too anything that you'd expect to be a positive trait if you are across the table from the wrong person.

Here's another example of how strange this world of business can be. While I was a tech writer, another tech writer discovered a *dirt file* on employees, supposedly hidden on a supposedly secure disk drive. This tech writer was smart, perhaps too smart for her own good. She cracked into this disk drive, which was ridiculously easy to do with that particular system, and printed off multiple copies of the dirt file. She left the copies on key managers' desks. Shortly after this episode, she was fired.

I bring this up as an introduction to what happened to me with another company. I quit my mainframe systems programmer job with this outfit to pursue a similar position with more responsibility in another state. Later, the first company moved a good portion of its midrange computing infrastructure to good old Colorado Springs, Colorado. This happened while I was working for MCI, before it was bought by WorldCom. I quit MCI to take the job with Memorial Hospital, also in Colorado Springs, and when that job became boring, I began exploring other opportunities nearby with a recruiting firm. One of the outfits that showed interest was the company that had moved in a few years before.

It looked as if an interview was going to happen, and I thought this would be good. I had left the old company without any hard feelings on either end. But much to my surprise and the recruiter's surprise, the company nixed the interview due to—get this—my moral values! What? I'd never had that one pulled on me, but obviously, the company keeps dirt files on its employees. What a rotten trick to play on someone. The speculations run wild when this happens.

Was it that I fudged on my English degree? No, that was discovered before or shortly after the job offer and was dismissed as being irrelevant to the job, or so I thought. The company first hired me to write procedure manuals for mainframe systems programming, and I was expected to grow into the status of a systems programmer while doing so. That can't be it.

Maybe it was the scandal that ensued after my leaving. The scandal involved my management and something to do with improper use of corporate funds, or so I had heard on the grapevine. Well, I had left before this scandal broke, and besides, I never got any crooked money from the company. Could someone over there at the Colorado Springs site be mistaken? Do they think I was in on that crime? Or am I guilty by association?

Another possibility came up: One of my former coworkers had taken a job with this company, and he probably got to review my resume. Did he sling mud at me? I don't know why he would if he did, but then who knows the evil that lurks in the hearts of men.

What a rotten thing for a company to do. There's no good reason for it other than someone over there is a nasty somonabitch, just like Gabby was with Johnny. By displaying behavior such as this, I have my doubts that I'd ever want to work for this company again. The politics must be very nasty, and who knows, maybe even crooked like the upper echelons of WorldCom were—and so many more corporate executives as we witness the criminals coming into the light. When someone accuses you of having bad morals, the chances are that a guilty conscious is talking. I guess this is one bridge that has been burned for me.

Times are tough when not enough jobs are available. Times are even tougher when trust is violated. I know I am guilty of petty misdemeanors involving the fudging of one credential, and maybe I am wrong to help Lydia with her classes, but to accuse someone of having bad morals without allowing this person to see and refute the evidence is a high crime covered by one of the Ten Commandments: Thou shalt not bear false witness against thy neighbors. Well, I am one of this company's neighbors, and it done me wrong.

I am sure you have your own stories of the crummy things that corporations can do to employees and former employees. During my more paranoid times, I suspect there might be a big dirt file database accessible by any major corporation considering any individual to hire. If this is so, then corporations, not the government, have destroyed the American Way. If this is so, we have all been reduced to the status of commodities, not individuals, not free people—we are reduced to sacks of brains and brawn to be traded on the free market.

During times when I am hopeful, which is most of the time, I know this isn't true, or if it is true, it makes no difference. We are free people and individuals because we choose to be, by our own free wills. When nasty things are done to us, we can make the choice to let it go and continue on as free people. Now, as the new year continues forward, let me—let us—make this choice to let it go and continue on.

What good does it do to carry a grudge? I'm as guilty as the next person when it comes to this, but it doesn't do me any good. In my family, as in Lydia's, as in anyone's, grudges can carry through for a lifetime. When Lydia's mother was on her deathbed, suffering from Alzheimer's disease, her hatred for her sister still burned in her soul. Lydia told me this, and because I trust her, I believe it to be true. Besides, I know my father and one of my aunts had issues that went back to the 1930s! Why? How can this carry on over decades?

Recent history has shown us that hatred among groups and individuals can carry on over centuries, even millennia. Are we doomed to hate? I sure hope not. I mean, even though I've also had long-term issues with some of my family members, I don't hate them for something that happened way back in childhood. I am crippled, though, for not having the ability to fully forgive, let it go, and move on. This is a tough issue.

Anyway, back to dirt files, crooked corporate executives, and accusations made without my having an opportunity to challenge them, or even know what they are. One corporation thinks I have bad morals, or at least someone within the corporation. And here I am writing about the situation. I suppose, if this ever gets published, that corporation might want to refute what happened—even deny that it ever happened. Yes, I would expect that, but listen: It doesn't matter. What does matter is that the accusation sent me into a tizzy of self-doubt. What does matter is how we handle such self-doubt, and my message to you is that we need to move on through self-doubt and into self-assuredness. This may involve all sorts of challenges, but the idea is that we have the power to decide to move on, no matter how badly we've been treated in the past.

The headlamps on the iron ore train can freeze us as it bears down. This is the most dangerous of situations, and something outside ourselves needs to knock us off the tracks. Then, once free of the fear-induced paralysis, we need to stick one foot in front of the other and move along our chosen paths. There will always be some obstacles to overcome, and our choice to overcome, or avoid, each obstacle is ours, and only ours. Nobody can make this decision for us, and more important, nobody can take this decision from us.

~ *9* ~

Working for a Living, Still Unemployed

Well, happy January 12! Yesterday, the guys came up and started building our new deck out back. Lydia had arranged this bit of improvement for the house before her pay at the University was cut in half. "Damn," she said, "I wouldn't have done this had I known." But, if we do need to sell the house, the new deck will help keep the price up there. Besides, I had a couple of royalty advance checks coming in for the book that would come to $4,000, so we could put part of that toward the $8,000 cost of the deck. In any case, the deck deal still goes on.

I don't know how this will change the bankruptcy. The deck will raise the appraised value of the house but maybe not by much. The housing market around here is very flat with lots of places on the market, but few are moving. Meanwhile, we definitely owe more than the limits set by law where if you have lots of equity in a place, you need to sell it to try to pay off creditors. This is one of those decisions that you don't know if it's right or wrong until the headlamps freeze you on the tracks. Then you have to decide whether to pull out or not. It's a lot like the coitus interruption method of birth control: Maybe you shouldn't go that way to begin with because pulling out will never feel right. In other words, were we wrong to buy this house when we did? How could we have known in 1998 that 2003 would be so bad? And now, should we proactively sell before my bankruptcy? Can we even sell with this flat market? Shoot, the tax value of the house has actually gone down! Well, I could never do the coitus interruption method of birth control, so I guess we just hang in here and see what cooks.

I've made a little more headway on another technical book about modeling grid computers. The main roadblocks involve trying to get modeling examples to compile and run with Java through Borland's JBuilder product. I'm using JBuilder because that is what the developers of the higher levels of modeling software used. I'm trying to be compatible here. The process is pretty slow at this stage of the game because so little is documented for newcomers like me. Oh, I know a lot about programming and object-oriented code, but there's always some little details that mean so much in the big picture. The same was true when I was learning SAS and MXG to do performance and capacity analysis on mainframes, back when I was in my late 30s. The tasks were full of twists and turns back then, and they still are today. I don't think we've come very far with making the development of code easier; it is just convoluted in different ways, which makes your early experiences less than valuable for figuring things out. About the only things you take with you are skepticism about documentation, skepticism about development environments, and a complete distrust of language vendors. Maybe the stupid code never did compile right—I hit that more than once with SAS and MXG, although on those platforms it was interpreted code. Some of the shipped code still did not interpret without errors, and they were pretty darn basic errors at that.

But I will prevail over Java, JBuilder, and grid modeling. You see, I am bull-headed and tenacious enough to expect this to work somehow. Once I get that down, then I can write about it so that other folks interested in doing grid modeling won't need to go through the first waves of pain. My genuine beliefs are that other techies will want this skill and that this skill will be in demand as the way corporations and other organizations' computing environments evolve into the next level. Why pay a bunch of money for your own computers when you can rent time on hundreds, thousands, maybe even millions of other computers as you need the time? And what if you could predict exactly how much any particular processing will cost? You can, of course, buy your own machines and make a private grid that is used more efficiently than anything available today. Or you could sell time on this private grid to others. This is a very old idea in computing: time sharing. Grids take the idea into its next level where literally every machine on a network, a set of networks, and even the Internet can all be used to do something useful. In business terms, this means making money or saving money. In scientific terms, it means expanding the idea of super computing into ultra-super-duper computing. You see, if you take 10 minutes of time on one computer and multiply the same 10 minutes by a thousand, you get 10,000 minutes of computing time that process in only 10 minutes of real time, because the thousand machines are all processing those 10 minutes *at the same time*. This is called *symmetrical multi processing*, or SMP. Thus, the work that once took nearly seven 24-hour days to process now could take only 10 minutes on a grid. You can see why many people in the higher echelons of business, computing, and science are all gaga over grid computing.

I am wondering if the government is as excited as we are (those of us who think this way). If it is, it sure doesn't show. George W. Bush is our president, and he seems to be more interested in waging war on Iraq and getting reelected than with anything else. Rumor has it that he is actually quite intelligent despite how he comes across on camera. I don't know. He seems to be like his father, George H. W. Bush, who had an astounding Zen experience with a grocery store scanning machine. I don't believe that the Bush family has ever been or ever will be much interested in computing technologies.

Don't get me wrong. Most people really don't care how computers work, just like most don't care how their cars, trucks, SUVs, ATVs, boat motors, leaf blowers, or government for that matter, work. Most people just want things to work, and that is that. Yet, there seems to be something about families. I come from a family in which the men, for the most part, cared how things worked because they needed to keep things working on their own. The men in my family generally don't make enough money to hire the work to be done, and so we have resurrected cars from junk yards, kept household appliances working far past their expected lifetimes, and pretty much thumbed our noses at planned obsolescence in a consumer-based economy. Our President does not come from such a family. The Bush family would rather tinker with socio-economic-military-international intrigues than change oil in the family sedan, although drilling for crude oil does seem to have something to do with the Bush family.

However you feel about this, the fact of the matter is that the government doesn't seem to care about moving the computing industry forward. Maybe it is just this period in history that has lost some vision. We seem to be focused on short-term business recovery and supplying the energy demand for the next fifty years or so. This brings me back to being unemployed and freelancing—did you think I forgot?

Both Lydia and I have a continuous dread of the future mixed with hopeful optimism that things will get better. Things can certainly get worse—of this we have no doubt. We may yet become homeless beggars. But we've successfully taken on a heavy load of University student papers for review, for pay. The pay is rather tiny at $3.75 per paper, but then we aren't giving any extensive English lessons either. Some students write fairly well while others do not. Most do not. Our experiences have shown us just how rare it is to find a good wordsmith and someone who can follow a style guide. It would help if the University were to settle on just one style. As it is, two are in use: APA and MLA. Fortunately, the differences have to do with paper format more than with straight grammar, punctuation, and style.

Some habits these students display are just downright annoying. Whoever taught them to use an apostrophe with a plural, non-possessive noun? What is up with those stray semicolons? Why is the comma, such an inexpensive commodity in writing, hardly ever used? (And why are so many parenthetical comments interjected when straight-up text would work just fine?)

Other habits are illuminating. We have known for a long time that people in general have abandoned reading for audio-visual entertainment. As a result, some students spell phonetically, which can result in some hilarious renditions of common phrases. We often quote these unintended and sometimes poignant mistakes to each other as we work. One woman had three groan men to supervise, while another student wrote about how God is omnipotent, omnipresent, and omnivorous. Since we occasionally enjoy a good steak with green beans and mashed potatoes, this reassured us of our diet's favor in the eyes of the Deity.

Both Lydia and I did our undergraduate work before the personal computer brought word processing to the masses. We typed our papers out on electric Underwood typewriters after hand-crafting the text on cheap notepaper. We kept three books handy whenever we wrote: a dictionary, a thesaurus, and the appropriate style guide. We used carbon paper to make two copies other than the original, and we used a chemical concoction of liquid paper to correct mistakes on the original. Because the physical writing process was such a drudgery, we composed our papers in our heads before ever putting pen to paper, and subsequently, fingers to typewriter.

Today, college students don't seem to benefit from the pressure to write in the imagination before tapping out thoughts on a computer keyboard. The lack of deep thought shows through as a result. We are wondering if a bachelor's degree now represents what a high school diploma once did, and if the master's degree is now only worth the old value of an undergraduate credential. It seems to us that the value of education has cheapened over the decades while the abilities of graduates to think, analyze, synthesize, and move forward with self-actualized knowledge into the harsh realities of modern life, and to gain greater wisdom from the experiences, has diminished. Are we becoming a highly educated society of freely thinking adults, or have we denigrated into ideologues who spout the conventional wisdoms of our prejudices, our faiths, and our personal political agendas? In the end, are we producing lazy thinkers?

Perhaps this is just old age criticizing youth or viewing current events through the gray-toned lenses of experience. What if one of my old college papers came through to me for review? Would I chuckle at the writing and, with a certain amount of smugness, pour electronic blue ink all over it? I have had over 25 years to improve my writing skills through my work and my reading. I am sure I've improved significantly along the way.

Other parts of the current college student experience actually make me a bit jealous. The introductory texts that students use for the University of Phoenix expose them to ideas that were radically new in the 1960s and 1970s. For example, the notion of becoming a lifelong learner is no longer something that long-haired intellectuals spoke of outside the hallowed walls of academia as a means for the lower middle, blue-collar working class to rise above mind-numbing factory labor. The notion of synthesizing ideas from research is no longer an exercise of intellect reserved for the blessed post-graduate students. Differences in learning style are acknowledged, as are the fundamental weaknesses of the lecture/note taking/test taking model. More emphasis is given to research and writing. More emphasis is given to thinking for yourself based on good logical analysis of published works, current event reports, and even the propaganda put out by various factions with special interests that don't necessarily keep the general interests in mind. Why, if I had the money, I'd want to finish up my bachelor's and go chase a master of some such subject in today's online university! But I'm unemployed and heading into bankruptcy. Perhaps this is me chasing my master's degree in hard knocks. This writing, then, is my master of hard knocks thesis.

Lydia has given me mercy on my duties to review student papers. After hearing my suffering moans and groans as I plodded through page after page of poorly constructed prose, day after day, and seeing how this drained me of the energy to write, she has restricted me to only a dozen papers per day, and only on days when she feels swamped. God, I love this woman!

Back when I was in college, I had a vague idea that I wanted to teach high school English and competitive speech forensics. Now I know that this would have been one of my biggest mistakes in life, due to the fact that bad prose makes me physically sick. I know this because, after reading three or four bad student papers, I need to read something good—a novel, a newspaper, a magazine article. Then, after recharging some sort of internal English grammar and punctuation battery, I can tackle another three or four bad papers. I'm just not an efficient editor, especially for writers who don't seem to have paid attention to basic grammar, punctuation, or know how to use a dictionary. Imagine my frustration if this was my full-time job with teenagers! It would have been a killer.

The good thing about this exercise is that I've tightened up my own grammar and punctuation. The bad thing is that my tightening up is also in the context of the formal English style that the University has embraced. Eh, so I use a lot more commas, semicolons, and colons than before, but now I can defend the usage with—tah-dah—The Holy Style Guide! Lydia even gives extra credit to her students if they can defend their grammar or punctuation, after being marked as incorrect, with style guide citations.

One of the hardest things I've had to master with reviewing (not grading) student papers is my tendency to comment on content. That is not my job, nor is it Lydia's for the straight grammar/punctuation/spelling/formatting editing that we do on papers that are not from Lydia's students. The students' professors have the responsibility to comment on content. But what do you do when a student writes about her abusive husband? Or a student expresses a great desire to learn more about computers, a field of expertise for me? How do you not comment when a good writer thinks he or she is a bad writer? This just yanks at our heartstrings when it happens.

So, once in a while, I sin. I avoid commenting on abusive spouses because I'm not a marriage counselor, but I have given some advice to the computer folks as to where to find more information on their interests, and I always tell a good writer that he or she is good and why. Lydia takes a look at my comments, takes out her magic Master's Degree Wand, blesses the comments, drives out my evil no-degree spirits, and off goes the paper to an appreciating student. Sometimes I sin, on purpose, because a greater good is served.

Ethics can be absolute or relevant to a particular situation. I'm not convinced that absolute ethics can ever work in the real world. I am convinced that those who promote such ideals are fooling themselves, and judging by the many self-proclaimed religious leaders who have fallen into disgrace through avarice or lust, or both, many innocents have been dragged down with them. In any case, I believe my sins are minor compared to the sins of the self-righteous. You may believe differently, and that's fine. It's your life and your relationship with your god, however you define that.

My God is omnivorous when it comes to sin.

I can say something else about writing and editing for a living, even though I'm not paid much for it yet: I like doing this more than anything else. Oh, I also like working with large computing systems, and that will probably be my path again once the economy turns around. I may even work on a master's degree in some field of computer technology, if ever I finish my bachelor's degree. But writing is in my blood. Ideas constantly flow into me most of the time. I dream about things to write, and my dreams often take the forms of scenes in a novel. The first thing I do upon awakening is to head for the computer, get online, check out a favorite political debate board, and write a few posts to the board. So, although the pay sucks right now, I enjoy what I do to make a living.

This points to something about career development and job hunting—you can be good at more than one thing. Because you can be good at more than one thing, you need to be wary of those who would put you into a tight little box with an overly restrictive definition. I'm not sure why some folks want to do this with other folks, but it seems to go along with tight little definitions of everything. I think some people need to compartmentalize everything, or else the world is just too chaotic to handle.

I once worked with another systems programmer who was like this. She was amazed that a technical writer could ever transition to a systems programmer. Why? Well, as her incantation went, technical writers use a skill set that is a lot different from a programmer's.

I asked her, "How is the skill set different? Don't both career paths involve abstract thinking? Don't both tasks involve understanding language syntax? Isn't visualization a big part of both jobs?"

I don't think she was ever convinced, even when I designed and built an online documentation system using the tools at hand. Sure, other documentation systems existed and had existed for some time, but this was my baby. I made it do what I wanted it to do.

Even when faced with undeniable empirical evidence, some people must deny reality because it doesn't fit into some preconceived cosmology. And so, we send out resumes that may have lots of experience and proof of the ability to pick up new skills rapidly, and a history of creative use of existing resources, but this doesn't sway the screeners who are looking for exactly the right mix of acronyms and recent experiences to fit the square hole they are attempting to fill. This kind of thinking drives me to distraction! But then, it is common, and I suppose it is a relatively safe way to think. If you have a square hole, why not look for a square peg?

How boring. Why not look for some Silly Putty that can transform to any shape of hole? What, your hole never changes shape? What kind of thinking is this? Denial of change in a chaotic, ever-changing world?

I call that "denial," it arises from "fear," and it does nothing to advance the corporation or the wise use of human resources. We are more like Silly Putty than square wooden pegs, and the square holes are more like clouds drifting in the sky than drillings in stone.

When hard economic times hit, people's minds seem to lock into the headlamps. All creative thought suspends, and worse, the mind stops thinking of real survival as the ore train bears down, steadily, rapidly, and with no regard for stupid deer caught in its gaze.

This is all a great challenge for serious job hunters and career changers. In a way, you have to shoot the buck's antler off, but instead of using a rifle, your weapons are self-analysis, self-awareness, solid direction, definite goals, knowledge, networks of people carefully and consciously constructed, and finally, solid reasoning with the person who has the power to hire you. We have to make our Silly Putty fit whatever cloud hole this person has.

Practicing what I preach, a job opportunity came my way from a contact I had made with a local company. I had left behind my published book and a packet of information about me containing my goals, skills, and supporting experiences. The slot was with marketing, and I'd be writing marketing documentation. In the course of the conversation, doubt arose that I really wanted to do this sort of writing.

I had to admit that I had little interest in marketing, other than for my own stuff, and so a key ingredient to the job offer stew was missing. I really didn't want the job. Now, about a month later, I am thinking of a different proposal. What if I wrote a commercial technical book about the company's products? Maybe this will work, and as soon as I get this book ready to sell, I'm going to pursue that idea.

So. The square hole was there but my Silly Putty didn't care. However, the clouds keep on changing—just keep looking for a more interesting hole to open up, or more likely, point out that an interesting hole is there for the filling.

~ *10* ~
Creative Visual Thinking

Today is Monday, January 13, 2003. We watched *60 Minutes* last night while enjoying a simple meal of hotdogs. The program presented two stories that at first inspired us but then, after thinking the ideas through, ticked both of us off.

The first story described how older Americans, people aging from around 65 to 90 years, had gone back to work in a factory setting. They produce medical needles, among other things. We reacted positively—hey, we are right in not worrying about retirement! Later, we became angry because only one professional was profiled, and he was a scientist. So, is the idea that we aging baby boomers are heading back to the factory work we rejected in our youths? I shuddered at the thought of doing brainless assembly work for a living. I'd rather do the student paper reviews—that at least keeps me sharp on grammar, punctuation, and to a much lesser extent, style. How can you improve your style by reading papers by students with writing problems? Well, I guess I do see what not to do, and I guess the whole situation does make me hungry for excellent writing. All right, style does improve through reading student papers.

The second story immediately disturbed us. It described how India has a university, IIT (Indian Institute of Technology), that is rated as perhaps the hardest university to attend and from which to graduate. Along with this message came the fact that many IIT graduates move to the United States to work, obtain citizenship, and in effect—as we thought—displace native high-tech workers. The problem isn't that either of us want to work in high-tech as engineers. No, we aren't cut of that cloth. The problem is with the H-1B visas and how the rules for foreign workers to obtain these visas could be bent to fit employers' desires. We assume employers want the cheapest labor they can get. We also assume that many of the jobs filled by H-1B visa holders could easily be filled by native workers who are unemployed, such as myself—if given a chance.

As the evening progressed, we started combining our observations and feelings, and we came up with this conclusion: The baby boomers are being set up to take menial jobs at minimum wages as we enter our 60s, 70s, 80s, and even 90s and beyond. The professions that we enjoy—systems administration/analysis and technology training/writing—will be shut out to us because of all these IIT graduates and H-1B visas! Why, it is a conspiracy!

After sleeping on this, I feel better about the whole concept. For one thing, ageism was being refuted by these folks who work in the medical needle factory. For another thing, the notion of retirement was being shown as something that kills you early if you need to be working to be active in both body and mind. Will we be forced to work menial jobs for minimum wage?

No, only if we want to do that. This principle of life has not changed: We do form our own destinies. My extended unemployment has given me the opportunity to break into technology writing and other forms of writing. Yes, the cash flow doesn't quite exist right now, but that will improve as we find more paying gigs and publish more books, articles, and the such. So let the graduates of IIT do the engineering work for hardware and software. What the hell, we don't want to do that anyway, and besides, I'll bet our own MIT and CalTech graduates will give the Indians a run for their money. What I want to do is write about grid computer modeling in a manner that cuts through the fog I have found surrounding this subject. I want to write so well that the IIT grads will be studying my text to figure out what the heck is going on. Over the years both Lydia and I have found that engineering types may be brilliant with various flavors of mathematics, but as writers they suck gooey offset printing ink. I don't think we have anything to worry about. As the economy recovers and the issues around war with Iraq take their courses, we will be able to increase our income back to where it once was and beyond.

At least that is the vision we have decided to embrace. I have come to the belief that we can form our own destinies through creative visualization. This idea came into my life through a friend who was also into reading Tarot cards. Initially thinking this was a bunch of new-age malarkey, I argued with her that no matter how much I visualize rolling in thousand dollar bills, it's never going to happen just by wishing it. She looked at me askance, a wry smile crinkling her cheek, and told me of course it won't happen. I had already argued myself out of it.

No matter how hard I tried, I could not believe in her ways until years later, after writing out career and personal goals, I reviewed those goals and realized that every single one of them had come true. Granted, I kept the goals from going over the top, like rolling in thousand dollar bills or being so filthy rich that I could afford a new Mercedes each year, but nevertheless, I had achieved goals that, at the time they were set, seemed very far away. Yet I believed that eventually I could achieve them, if only I did the required steps to reach those goals.

One of those requirements is creative visualization of attaining the goal. What would it feel like? What things might happen? Among these goals, I had set out to make $75,000 per year. At the time I was making about $40,000. This goal was achieved a year and a half before my layoff, so maybe I should have made it seventy-five grand and above for an extended period of time. Do you think? Eh, I don't know. Maybe I should have.

During the last year of my employment, I was desperately trying to find some new direction, some new goal, to achieve. I felt that I had reached the top of my game as a systems administrator and was losing interest in expanding that role. Although I enjoyed my work when busy, the amount and scope of projects had dwindled. Work was becoming rote, mundane, repetitive, and I was heading into boredom. This is never a good thing for my type.

So one afternoon, I was chatting with another systems administrator, and he started in on a story about the Alaskan Highway. It struck me then, hey! Why don't I plan an extended motorcycle trip on my dual-sport and do the Alaskan Highway? Sure. I can take fifty days off, starting on my fiftieth birthday, which was about a year away at that time, and *write about the experience!*

Uh-oh, I was in trouble then! I had just visualized a goal, and I believed in the goal, and by gosh the goal would be met. The trouble is, the actual motorcycle trip has not taken place, and I will probably turn fifty-one before the money is available to make this happen. So what? Why not *fifty-one days for fifty-one years?* Sure, and if that doesn't work out, fifty-two days for fifty-two years. Shoot, this could even become seventy days for seventy years!

But you see what has happened. I have become a published writer. That part of the visualization has come to pass, and I'll bet, because of my long-term time requirements for the motorcycle trip and the reluctance of employers to grant me that much time off, I must figure out how to be an independent writer. I can't work for an employer any longer!

Both a blessing and a curse, I think that I am stuck. Maybe I could change visions? But why if the first vision is working out, and it does seem to be? I'm even suspecting that I've signed some sort of spiritual contract on this. Once headed down this path, I have to see it to completion.

Lydia talks about this a lot, too. She believes strongly that we have to go through stages in life, and that if we try to shortcut a stage, we end up doing it later on and with possibly a lot more pain than if we had simply done it while younger. I imagine that might be true, at least for people like us.

Regardless of that, along with creative visualization comes writing. Writing out goals—and the more detailed the better, you don't want to make my earnings mistake—has some kind of magic to it. If you do the career development work, you'll be writing a lot. One of the exercises I remember was to list all the things you want in your new job and career in one column, and then alongside that column, list all the things you don't want. Goal setting goes both ways, what you want and what you don't want.

For example, I had listed "Working with highly talented, smart people" as one of my wants, and "No jerks" as one of my don't wants. For the most part, this has come true. Had I been more specific with the term *jerks*, maybe I wouldn't have had to work with a couple of difficult types I encountered in my career. They aren't jerks exactly. Just difficult in some ways, but otherwise truly talented and smart. So again, try to be as specific as you can. The spirits have a great sense of humor.

My visualized motorcycle trip has taken on a number of modifications. I no longer want to do the Alaskan Highway because, after reading some books on the subject, I realize that this is no longer a very interesting thing to do on motorcycle.

Before the road had been paved, this trip was quite a challenge for four-wheel drive vehicles and motorcycles. Now, massive motor homes can easily make the trip. As a result, I'm thinking that the trip should be along the northwestern back roads of the United States and Canada with no particular goal at all. I want to just let the experiences happen and document them as I go, which is the way I took my other extended motorcycle trips. The exception is that back then, I had no intention of writing about travel on two wheels. Plus, all the trips were done by road bike and within three weeks.

Thinking back to those earlier motorcycle days, I did have a strong desire to somehow combine motorcycling with the way I made my income. Huh! How about that. It looks like my creative visualizations have a history.

When you set out to determine and write your goals, you might as well think big. What the heck, if you have the courage and determination to do what needs to be done, why not? I doubt Bill Gates started Microsoft with the idea that all he wanted was a little business that would pay the bills and provide a comfortable living. I bet Mr. Gates had his sights set on becoming the IBM of the PC world, and sure enough, Microsoft is now big, powerful, and has several de facto standards in the software world.

One of the best systems of setting goals I've encountered is produced by the FranklinCovey company. In this system, you start with values, work toward goals that support those values, and then keep track of what you do on a daily basis to achieve those goals. I tried this for several years and then abandoned the methodology because, for me, it became too much work to keep track of all the things I do to work toward my goals. Maybe I had internalized the methodology, or maybe I just got lazy. In any case, if you're having trouble setting goals and working toward them, this might be just the system for you.

I'm visualizing that pile of thousand dollar bills. Oh, they smell so sweet. Fresh off the presses, crisp, clean, and so many of them! I'm seeing a fat balance in a bank account. Is all that really mine to do with as I please? I'm sitting down to write out payoff checks to all my creditors. The balance isn't even dented, and what's this? It seems to be actually growing!

Now I'm at the motorcycle dealership picking out a brand new dual-sport. Something in red maybe? Something more road worthy than what I have, but can still handle rough dirt roads? Yes, and perhaps a set of hard saddlebags.

Fast forward to the fifty-something days for fifty-something years trip. It is morning. I'm drinking coffee fixed over a small propane camp stove. The morning sun is rising above a big river, the birds are singing, and the air smells sweet with wildflowers and pine. Finishing my coffee and stuffing the cup into my packs, I mount my trusty dual-sport and ride off to the north and west along a smooth dirt path that leads me to this day's adventures.

I like creative visualization. It can be a lot of fun when you really believe these things will come true.

I don't know what to say to doubters. I was there once, and I think all my argument against the validity of creative visualization kept me down for many years. This stretch of unemployment has been hard on my faith, too, but maybe it was necessary to knock me off the old, boring tracks and onto a new path in life. Think I'll visualize that for a while.

~ *11* ~

Tragedy and War

Yesterday, February 1, 2003, the space shuttle Columbia broke apart during reentry. I was up early and listening to NPR when the news reports started to come through. Lydia came down here to my writing area to open up the garage door using the opener we keep near the French doors. It was Saturday morning, and that meant that the deck people would be here to do their weekend construction work. That's when I told her about the tragedy, but she wasn't very much awake and just shook her head as she went back upstairs to start her day.

Once the radio broadcasts started to repeat, I turned on the TV down here and caught those reports. As the day progressed, I became busy with reviewing university papers and dealing with what seemed like a system problem at the university. Lydia speculated that they had lost a T1 line because our uploads were moving extremely slow, taking hours to get just one reviewed paper back to the system. I shrugged. It could have been anything, but it wasn't us because we could get to other sites just fine.

The five o'clock news reported that Iraq thought the tragedy was God's punishment for the US. Someone was trying to sell pieces of Columbia on eBay. President Bush gave his condolences, looking like he was having one of the worst days of his life. Did I detect a bit of glaze in his eyes—did he feel caught in the headlamps?

This morning I have put my daily worries away and composed this poem:

Faulty O-rings or a nicked wing, it all leads to the same damn thing. Courage knows no particular nation, sex, or race. We die as we have lived, Some more significantly than others. I don't feel punished but honored To have been given this reminder during these hard scrabble days: Life is to be lived with courage. Anything else is wasting time.

We seem to be a nation that responds to threats from terrorists and rogue nations only with fear. We are wasting our time doing this because, first off, we are creating future terrorists, as is to be expected when one nation attacks another. So we are perpetuating foreign policy based upon fear. Right now the push is on to take out Saddam Hussein, his cronies, his generals, maybe even his clerics. I, along with a lot of other folks, think that oil has a lot to do with this push. I, along with a lot of other folks, believe this war isn't worth the initial expense in terms of human lives and tax dollars, nor is it worth the payback in terms of more highly motivated terrorists trying to mess us up in whatever ways they can dream up. We could very well be wrong, but doggone it, the leap from attacking Afghanistan to take out Osama bin Laden and al Qaeda to attacking Iraq just doesn't follow. The rationalizations to attack Iraq seem to have been dreamt up as we went along. First it was connections to terrorism. That didn't fly, and next it was concern about weapons of mass destruction. Then North Korea kicked up its heels, and now we want Iraq to disarm completely or else!

On the 15th of February, a peace rally is scheduled to be held in Colorado Springs. I plan to go with my camera and little tape recorder with the intent of writing freelance articles from the grist I collect. After being in the headlamps for more than a year, I am tired of it. I am tired of feeling panicked all the time, tired of hearing about more layoffs at WorldCom and others, tired of considering myself unemployed.

As of now, I am employed: I am self-employed and will behave as such. I am a self-employed freelance writer. I am no longer an unemployed systems administrator.

The iron ore train chugs on by. The deer looks over his shoulder a moment, and then back to the trail before him. He walks on, never looking back.

Well, I went to the peace rally. Some of it was fun, and I wrote up an article, as follows:

Peace Rally in Militaryville

On Saturday, February 15, 2003, thousands of Coloradans gathered together in common protest against the impending war with Iraq. The rally organizers chose Colorado Springs for this gathering, home to the Air Force Academy, Fort Carson, NORAD, Peterson Air Force Base, Schriever Air Force Base, and the recently formed U.S. Northern Command. According to the website www.coloradosprings.com, in 2001 the military brought $2.67 billion in revenue to the local economy and employed 41,672 people, of which 29,218 were active-duty personnel and cadets. The rest were civilians. One out of three adult residents depended on the military, and this number may be higher today as the private economy suffers while the military builds up. When taken as a whole, the military is Colorado Springs' largest employer, and the town stands as a symbol of American military strength. This is exactly why the organizers chose Colorado Springs for the rally.

Saturday was cold. Freezing fog pervaded the canyon as I guided my Jeep down from the small mountain town of Woodland Park. Low gray skies loomed over Colorado Springs as I traversed the streets to my destination: Palmer Park, right at the intersection of Academy Boulevard and Maizeland Avenue. Stage hands and sound people were setting up. The rally would not start for another hour, and so I found a parking spot near the stage and read background literature.

The primary rally organizer was CCAWI (Colorado Coalition Against the War on Iraq, www.ccmep.org/ ccawi.htm). People from all around the state were invited to attend, but as the crowd grew over the next hour, and once the speaking started, most had come from Boulder—at least so I thought during that early part of the morning. If Colorado Springs represents the conservative military, Boulder represents liberal intellectuals.

I listened to the first two speakers, who listed all the reasons why the US has become a slave to the military-industrial complex, what has been happening in Iraq since Desert Storm, and what war in this region will bring to the US and the world. No new arguments were put forth. Many Iraqis—children mostly—have died due to UN sanctions; war will result in many more Iraqi deaths; war will destabilize the region; war will encourage terrorists; war is not the answer. The military is huge; the military is secret; the military is doing many things against the best interests of US citizens and citizens of the world. Although I had not attended a peace rally since the Vietnam era, much of the rhetoric had not changed. One thing was missing that had been commonplace at Vietnam rallies: the smell of burning marijuana. This was a clean crowd of concerned, law-abiding citizens.

The day was not warming up. I retired to the Jeep and its heater for a break. The crowd was steadily growing.

Stalking its periphery, I struck up several conversations with people. Yes, a good turnout. How many do you suppose? Oh, three, maybe five thousand. Millions of people are protesting worldwide, you know. Bush has got to get this message. But he will have his war; he doesn't care what we think. We don't need all this oil! It's for the oil, you know. War sucks. There's got to be a better way. What's the alternative for war? Oh, you know that—it's peace! Peace starts in your heart. Peace comes about one heart at a time. We ought to be developing alternative energies like solar and wind! Why do we continue to use so much oil?

I thought back to a puppet show that a theater group from Boulder did at the beginning of the rally. The puppets were large, painted, papier-mâché affairs put over people—Bush a 10-foot boar and Hussein a 10-foot snake. Shorter living puppets milled about: a jogger with headphones, someone talking on a cell phone, one with an attaché case. The boar and snake fought a war of words, as sung to well-known popular melodies from top-40 charts long past, as the inconsequential puppets went about their jogging, talking, and other self-absorbed interests.

The UN doesn't matter. George will have his war no matter what! He has already declared this; we have no reason to believe he might change his mind. Why did he push for war before the 2002 elections? To win Congress, of course! Just look at the huge buildup of troops since then!

I asked if this rally and the other rallies around the world were just exercises in futility then. Why protest if it won't do any good?

A very old woman, hunched over and breathing oxygen through a tube, looked up at me with kind, bright blue eyes: "We must because we can still do this."

Indeed. Will homeland security eventually include a ban on protest? Pondering this possibility, I ambled toward Academy Boulevard where protesters were beginning to line up to solicit horn toots and sympathy for the cause. A 30-something man caught my eye, perched on a split-rail fence, dressed in ski gear, a walking staff propped against his leg. We chatted.

He lived in Woodland Park too, on the other side of town from me. Yes, we had seen each other around town—in the grocery store, at Tres Hombres (a Texas-styled road house with tasty Tex-Mex food, good live music, fairly cheap beer), and other little places about town. Jeffrey, my fellow Woodland Park resident, is an observer. He saw factions within the protesters.

"There are the troublemakers," he pointed out, "the ones with black flags and black bandanas pulled up over their noses, as if they were bandits."

"Yeah," I agreed, "those are the rowdies. If trouble happens, they will instigate it."

Jeffrey and I griped about the bad economy for a while, and then I left to join the line of protesters.

Horns honked, peace signs flashed, a few motorists flipped half-signs (middle fingers) and shouted, "Get a grip!" Most drivers were stoic as they passed by. The police shut down the street from traffic and routed drivers around the rally. Then they opened it up for a while, only to shut it down again. What fun is this when you don't have an audience?

The police opened up the street again. It seemed that the point had been made, and the energy of the crowd started to fade. No war. No war. No war. You get tired of saying it over and over again.

I needed to pick up materials from a couple of library branches around town, so I headed off to do those errands. One branch was south and the other east. After visiting the south library, I headed back to Academy Boulevard on my way to the east branch. The street had been closed again, and I was routed around the rally. Darn it, I wanted to toot my horn in support! I wanted to flash a full, two-fingered peace sign! I assumed the police had decided that the peace rally was over.

Later that evening, I caught the local news. The peace rally had turned "ugly" toward its end, as put by the news anchor who wore a concerned look. Police made arrests and used tear gas.

I found out that the police had launched a tear gas canister into a parking lot where people were not moving out as directed. Civil disobedience? Police overreaction? I suppose this will be argued over in letters to the editor and perhaps an editorial or two. Well, maybe the black bandanas got out of hand. They did seem to be potential troublemakers, but something did not seem right: What was the big deal about a parking lot?

While at the east library branch, I wore two not-war buttons on my long coat. After gathering my books and while approaching the end of the line for checkout, a man about my age spotted the two buttons. He looked at me with shocked eyes. Is it back? Are we doing this again? He avoided my eyes. Yes, this is happening again, but this time it is different. Our motivations for carrying out the war on Iraq are in question before the attack begins. With Vietnam, it took years after the war began for peace rallies to gain any momentum, and then a lot of them were treated as mere excuses to party. Just about all the protesters were young college students.

This time around, we who protest are an eclectic group representing all ages and a broad spectrum of professions. We reject violence for the purpose of gaining press coverage. We reject the use of alcohol and illegal drugs.

We guess at the underlying motivations, and as with all speculation, we really don't know. We are probably wrong, mostly, but what are the real reasons to wage this war? The very fact that the real reasons are not up for discussion indicates to me that they are too cynical and self-serving for public discourse. This leads us to think the worse: The war is only for oil. It is for the profit of large corporations. The Bush administration is crazy.

Meanwhile, the real reasons may have longer-term rationales to bring peace to the Middle East. The chilling part of this speculation is that thousands of lives, Iraqi and American, must be sacrificed to bring about a greater good. It had better be very much a greater good, too, because otherwise we are citizens of a country worthy of the world's contempt and hatred.

This peace rally has the distinction of being the only peace rally in the world to have been gassed that day. Sure enough, a lot was written about the police gassing the crowd. Naturally, people landed into two camps: those who condemned the police action and those who defended it.

I'm finishing this chapter as the war in Iraq comes to the end of the shooting part. Fortunately, not many American lives, and not nearly as many Iraqi lives as I thought before, have been lost. I am so grateful that the worst possible scenario—the use of chemical, biological, or even nuclear weapons—did not happen. I think we were all holding our breath through this whole thing.

Some of the war supporters have gloated over being right about war in Iraq. Just look what a resounding success it has been! Well, yes, the shooting war was blessedly short, and Iraq did not use the weapons of mass destruction it is supposed to have. Why was that? Aren't there any? The search goes on to find them, and I have no doubt that they will be announced as found, whether they were really there before the war or not. It seems like a moot point now.

The only reason I bring the tragedy of the shuttle disaster and the war in Iraq up is that these two events shocked and stunned me into inaction for a period of time. I regressed to those feelings of being useless, unemployed, good for nothing, and hopeless. Maybe the economy is still in such bad shape because we are all shell shocked? How many tragedies can we put up with? Are we to now do war with Iran, North Korea, Syria, or who? When will this all blow up in our faces?

It amazes me how many people put their trust into the Bush administration, and perhaps their trust is well-founded. I just wish I knew what that foundation is. It seems to be built only upon the fact that this is a Republican administration, and as everyone knows, Republicans are right. Ha-ha.

People who lived through the Vietnam era tend not to have so much trust. We know how badly the government can lie to us, straight-faced, repeatedly, and with no apology when the lies were exposed. Rather, a greater effort to keep the voices of dissent down went into play, culminating in the shooting of students at Kent State.

Well, the Vietnam war finally did end as our troops evacuated in great haste and under enormous stress. Saigon and South Vietnam fell.

I just hope our government is trying to be as straightforward with us as it can right now. I think with all the trust put behind this administration, it would be political suicide if lies are being constructed, only to be revealed by someone trying to make a name for him or herself.

I feel that something bigger than us is going on. The smell of big change is in the air, like smoke from a wildfire. It is too early to tell if the Iraq war will ultimately be successful in its aftermath of building a democratic nation, but other things have come out. More layoffs have been announced and more corporations have been caught with cooked books, and none of this is good news for the economy.

I'm working double time to finish this book because I have other projects I want to start. The book on grid computing is still alive, but during my research into other subjects, I came across an interesting view of ecologists and environmentalists. I want to pursue that topic and write about it. Some events are coming this summer that I want to cover for possible articles to sell. Then there's the local company that might be interested in helping me to produce another technology book. I'm about to get very busy.

Another feeling I have is that a lot of other people are getting busy, too. Something's in the air. Something's definitely in the air.

~ *12* ~
Freely Freelancing

How long can this go on? Good morning, it is now the seventh of March, 2003. I have been unemployed for one year and just a little over four months. We are about to go to war with Iraq, and the buildup to this war has been in the making for, what, half a year?

Last night, our president, George Walker Bush, put on what seemed to me to be a scripted press conference in which he informed us, in contrite words, that gosh darn it, we have no choice but to blow the shit out of Iraq. You know, because they might blow the shit out of us someday. Meanwhile, the North Koreans are about to blow the shit out of everybody.

A generation or three ago, we joked about what a mad, mad, mad world this is. Yeah? Well now we have a crazy world. It is a god forsaken crazy world. Insane. Nothing makes sense any longer, and we are, I think, pretty much fed up with this crap.

I've never liked Bush, but now I really don't like him. He is sending a couple hundred thousand of our regular troops and hired contractors (need to learn more about this) into Iraq to take out one guy and a handful of his henchmen. Maybe a few thousand of his special, loyal troops. But I don't hate President Bush.

No, not like I hated Richard M. Nixon or Lyndon B. Johnson when the Vietnam war was going on. Those guys were personal to me—as if I knew them. I don't know Bush. I feel he lives in one universe while I live in another. You have to feel you know these people before you can hate them. With Bush, I just don't care—I just don't like him, a whole lot. I wish he would go back from whence he came.

A few weeks ago I went to that peace rally in Colorado Springs with the intention of writing an article about the experience. Well, I wrote the article and tried to sell it to *The Nation*, but nothing came of the effort, I suppose because it really did turn out to be a big story. You see, of all the hundreds of peace rallies that went on worldwide, only the town of Colorado Springs had any trouble worth talking about. And I had left the rally too early to see any of the trouble. Damn! What kind of freelance journalist am I, anyway? No nose for news.

I arrived at the site of the peace rally early on that cold, overcast mid-winter day. The crowd gradually built as speakers spoke about peace, war, the military-industrial complex, how we build peace one heart at a time, and so on. I went into the crowd and just struck up casual conversation randomly. First, a retired high school history teacher who was pushing alternative energy sources like generating electricity from the wind. Then some young people, maybe college kids or recent graduates, at one of the information (slash) fund-raising tables. Somebody a few decades older than me. A Vietnam War vet. High school kids making their protest signs. Pretty much anybody who wanted to chat.

The rally went on, people lined up along a busy street, and I went off to pick up some library books. Ho hum, I thought, not much news at this rally. But while I was off doing my errands, something newsworthy did happen. The Colorado Springs police decided to shoot tear gas into the crowd.

That made news. It raised a stink. Editorials, letters to the editor, and television news covered the event. The ACLU is looking into a deeper investigation. Dirty laundry will be aired.

Unless all this gets censored as we head off to war.

What the hell is going on with the press these days? Last

night's news conference was scripted. Bush knew who was going speak, what order each person was to stand up and yammer out a pansy-ass question, and he may have even known what the question was going to be. Where were the tough journalists who ask the hard questions? Nowhere. I felt like I was an Iraqi citizen watching my all-powerful leader do yet another meaningless propaganda speech. Well, no, it isn't that bad—yet. I felt like I was being pimped one more time by a guy I don't like, don't respect, and don't believe he is actually in my universe. I didn't vote for him last time, and I am really not going to vote for him this time.

I am going to vote Democrat or maybe third party. I don't care who is running.

Ah, but my sort-of-important vote for president doesn't get maybe-counted for another nineteen months. Is this enough time for this war on Iraq to get started, ended, and for the democracy to be set up? Will all this be finished by Election Day?

Maybe. And you know what? I bet the guy gets reelected. I bet that because the propaganda machine is very powerful. It has convinced the American public that 1) It is cool to be conservative 2) Nobody can tell us what to do 3) We don't have to worry about conserving energy 4) We don't have to worry about conserving water 5) We should consume as we want 6) Liberals are evil.

I heard today that about 300,000 jobs were lost last month (February, 2003). That's what the population of Colorado Springs was—before a bunch of people got laid off and had to leave the state, looking for work—any kind of work. We have also lost 2,000,000 jobs over the past two years. I think that's about the population of Denver and its suburbs. It's definitely around the population of a small country.

The old panicked feeling is back, but this time it doesn't seem to have anything to do with being unemployed. I feel employed, although the pay is really bad. If I am not reviewing student papers, then I'm writing lectures or writing on this and other books. I've also been trying to do articles on various events, as mentioned earlier regarding the peace rally. This means that I'm paying attention to what goes on around me and what might be happening in the near future.

One thing that will be happening on March 25th is a symposium about whether business can achieve better energy efficiencies, to be hosted by the Rocky Mountain Institute near Vail, Colorado. I recently discovered this place while doing some research on energy policies, but it has been in existence for about twenty years. In any case, I plan to attend and write up another article. That will make three that I've tried to publish.

Since I've jumped out of the headlamps and onto the freelance writing trail, I've not abandoned my job search. I know it will take a lot of effort and perseverance to become published again, whether this turns out to be a book or an article. Putting one foot in front of the other, I move ahead.

Blam, Boom, Wham! The war in Iraq has ended. We haven't found any weapons of mass destruction yet, but oh what the hell, we're easy. Seems that 60% of us as of now, May 5, 2003, don't really care. We are now to pay attention to the economy and all the corporate crooks who have been coming from under rocks, even as the war grabbed all headlines.

All right, let's get this economy going! How? Tax cut! Oh.

I'm still thinking that someday I will be working again. You know, at a real job? Get a paycheck every two weeks, hand most of it over to Lydia for expenses and to help pay down the debt she has incurred over the unemployment period. (She has decided not to do bankruptcy.) This thinking is hard to shake when you're about midway along a new path. It's like when I transitioned from the warehouse to technical writing. After three years of tech writing, I found myself looking for a new job. Know what? I still answered ads for warehouse workers. Then, after transitioning to systems programmer, I still answered ads for tech writers. Even during this long, interminable unemployment stint, I've answered ads for tech writers.

But now I am a writer. I am a writer. I am a writer. If I keep saying this enough times, maybe I'll start to believe it. Maybe I should call myself an author instead? Let's try that out: I am an author. I am an author. I am a broke author living off the kindness of my loved one, a gigolo, a bum, a loser, STOP!

See how hard it is to cast off the old baggage? I'm still checking the job wanted ads for systems administrators, tech writers, and anything else I might be able to fit into. It's as if I can look back to the railroad tracks from where I am through the magic of the Internet, and I yearn for what once was. I've forgotten how bored I had become with that old path. I've forgotten that I had reached the end of the old path.

I did go to the symposium on how business can be worked to be more ecologically friendly. I wasn't impressed. The Coca-Cola company tightens up the pipes in its plants to reduce water leaks. Gee. A small bakery uses organically grown wheat flour. Dang. No, there was nothing newsworthy about this thing. Then I went to visit The Rocky Mountain Institute, a building designed to be very energy efficient. That was a bit more interesting, but the place seemed to be a little rundown, and the self-guided tour sent me off into nowhere. I think it was the fourth sign that pointed me down a path that ended at a gravel road. I lost interest.

A visit to the HyperCar office was also a disappointment.

The HyperCar was supposed to be a hybrid SUV that could get astounding gas mileage, around 80 miles per gallon, but all that they had was two nonworking models, one small and one full scale. Development on the HyperCar had stopped due to the enormous amount of money it takes to build something like this. Now the outfit works on developing composite materials and design ideas for the existing automotive industry. I lost interest.

Being a writer, though, I could not let this trip become a waste. What else is there to write about regarding ecology? I started to explore the local library for books on the subject. First, energy. How do we produce our energy? Well, we burn a bunch of coal to generate around 50% of our electricity. This amounts to just under two trillion kilowatt hours (KWH) per year. Nukes generate just under 800 billion KWH, 600 billion for natural gas, just over 200 billion for hydro, about 125 billion for petrol, and last and least, 80 billion KWH for renewable, non-hydro power. Everything trends upward except petrol and hydro, probably due to cost and drought.

Of the renewable, non-hydro power, solar is last, wind is next to last, geothermal comes next followed by burning waste, and wood burning comes in with the most electricity generated, a paltry 40 billion KWH (source: www.doe.gov).

Does the fact that we burn enough coal each year to generate two trillion KWH disturb you? I found this to be somewhat interesting. That's a lot of coal! Where does it all come from?

West Virginia, to be sure. Montana and Wyoming, yep. But where else? I dug up more information, and it seems that 38 of the 50 states have significant coal reserves. We have an estimated 4 trillion tons of coal, with 296 billion tons recoverable using today's technology (source: **www.alrp.com**).

So, what does this mean? I guess it means that the coal

industry doesn't want to hear anything about carbon dioxide emissions causing global warming. I mean, if we burn coal in the most efficient and clean way possible, we still get a lot of carbon dioxide from the combustion. Well, this could be something to write about!

After doing a lot more research, I discovered that this has already been written about, perhaps to excess. I need a different angle to approach ecology. This is an ongoing thing for me, but the point is that writing is becoming a lot more fun than when I first started. Even with war and rumors of future wars running around in Armageddon fashion, I can still stick one foot in front of the other and move ahead. Hey, what's the worst that can happen? The end of the world? I guess employment then becomes a moot point.

~ *13* ~
Not as Simple as We Thought

Today is the last day in March, 2003. We had a big snowstorm a while back, and still snow hangs on, melting slowly, getting recharged with smaller snowfalls that piddle and spit from visiting clouds. The war goes on into, what is it now, the twelfth day? Somehow it seems longer than that.

The Iraqi people have been putting up more of a fight than was expected. This is looking like a tougher war than what was promised, although I don't think anything was really promised. Everybody for the war had their fingers crossed. Meanwhile, people are dying to promote a cause that I don't believe is the real reason for this war: the liberation of Iraq. Americans are dying and Iraqis are dying. If not dying, then expecting to or living with damage both physical and psychological. Why did anyone believe this war would be different from any other war?

I'm old enough to remember Vietnam and how Lyndon Banes Johnson would appear on television with his heavy heart to ask for another bunch of troops for that crazy Asian war. My brother, Rick, went—and he was lucky to have returned with relatively minor damage. The draft back then kept changing the rules. At first you could be exempted if you had a family. Then that changed. Rick had a family, but I guess it wasn't old enough or something. Back then I was only around sixteen years old, not very aware of details, and dealing with my own adolescent problems.

Rick came back home just before Christmas of 1969. I was a senior in high school dating Mary Kay and wondering about my chances with the draft. Nobody wanted to get drafted.

Antiwar sentiment had grown strong. The original goals of the war were dim memories—what were they, anyway? Stop communism from spreading? Was that it? Did we care what government Vietnam had? What was the threat to the United States?

I had a conservative friend, Dave. Dave talked positively about the war but never joined to fight. He went on to college to earn an engineering degree and wound up working for some mining outfit. We crossed paths a few times after high school, but we never kept in touch over all these years. I wonder if he is the same now, you know, conventional? It's hard to imagine remaining the same; however, I know how some people think, and being conservative became cool with Ronald Reagan and others. Conservative to me means being against socialism, for tax cuts, for free trade, and against government regulation of business. It can also mean being conventional: accepting whatever the Republicans say and deriding anything the Democrats say. It's like a religion. I suppose those on the left wing of things are the same. I'm sort of over there with the ecologists, socialists, and bleeding hearts.

Dave and I took a motorcycle trip during the late summer of 1971. We both had Honda 450s. His had high pipes and braced handlebars, a model called a *scrambler* back then. Mine was the low pipe street model. Scramblers were supposed to be suitable for dirt riding, but everyone knew it was just a style statement. True dual-sport motorcycles like the one I ride today were not to be on the market for years to come. So Dave rode the "redneck" bike style, and I rode the "hippie" style. We were neither redneck nor hippie, but there was enough personality differences to make the trip stressful at times.

This was really Dave's dream trip. He had it all planned out. I was just along for the ride, but this trip opened me up like nothing could have. We started out early on a cool August morning, heading northward into Canada. Our packs were loaded with all sorts of things we would not need, and so the bikes were a tad difficult to handle in soft sand. Going through a construction area, we dumped a few times—but at slow speeds, so we didn't hurt ourselves or the bikes.

Passing through the border at International Falls, we enjoyed the scenic King's Highway, Number 1, through Kenora and Winnipeg. In my childhood, my folks would take the family to vacation up there. Then we scooted ever westward through Manitoba, Saskatchewan, and into Alberta toward the Canadian Rockies. Neither of us had ever seen a mountain.

The highway became a long, straight ribbon flanked by sunflower fields in full bloom and preparing for harvest. We could see the curvature of the earth as mile after mile slipped beneath us. A hornet got stuck in Dave's helmet. I wondered what was up with him as suddenly he ripped his helmet off, shook his head wildly, and slowed to pull over. We took a break then as Dave applied salve to his burning neck.

I remember looking around and feeling both isolated and free. What an immense place this earth of ours is! Home was hundreds of miles back, and the Pacific Coast another bunch of miles ahead. Back in Winnipeg we had jettisoned some of the useless stuff we had packed, but we still had enough to stay fairly comfortable through the cooling nights of late August.

One evening as we sought out a campground, two Canadian bikers linked up with us. They told us that the nearest campground was a long way down the road, and that we'd need to ride through part of the night. Dave and I didn't like that idea. We would just sleep by the side of the road. The Canadians looked at us aghast—why, that's against the law! Or was it the rules? I don't quite remember, but we thought nothing of laying out sleeping bags a little distance off the highway. However, the Canadians seemed to think it was the equivalent of bank robbery. Was that a cultural thing? Americans don't fear the rules as much as Canadians? To appease our Canadian friends, Dave and I took a side road and found a secluded place to lay out our bags. Our Canadian friends jammed on toward the campground way down the darkening road, the taillights of their BMWs winking out over a distant hill.

We had been out for five days when the mountains started to show on the horizon. At first they appeared to be nothing more than a cloud bank, but as we came closer, the foothills gained definition and height. We were soon climbing into the high country of Alberta.

Minnesota isn't exactly flat, but its hills and bluffs are nothing compared to real mountains. We guided our mounts through twisting roads and gawked at snowcapped peaks all around. How rugged and primeval these mountains felt! How crisp and fresh the air tasted! We stopped often to soak it all in.

Near Banff, we took a little side trip to see more of the magnificence that God had created. We came upon an A-frame house where a woman, somewhere around middle age, waved to us, beckoning. She had locked herself out of her house and wanted help getting back in. We stopped to lend a hand.

After boosting her to an unlocked window through which she crawled, the woman opened her door and invited us in. She made us some herbal tea and started rambling about this and that while describing how the spiders were bad this time of year. She'd been bitten several times. As her talk took us from subject to subject, we both realized that the woman was a bit crazy. Maybe schizophrenic because some of her stories had to do with being watched by government agents. We politely said goodbye and headed back to the highway.

I think the mountains can make you crazy if you don't have companionship. I do have a loner streak in me, but not to the point where I could be a hermit. Maybe living alone in the mountains can bring you closer to God, but maybe that closeness is too much to handle for most folks. I've known solitude in the hills, and it is a richly intense sort of peace that can lead to seeing all things differently. It can also bring on mirages and hallucinations to where you wonder what is real and what is illusion. Maybe this can lead to some sort of enlightenment where the spiritual path becomes the only path. I don't know, but I have seen that it could lead there, and I have gained a little enlightenment in the mountains.

Going back into these memories is comforting at this time. It makes me want to ride off into the hills on my dual-sport motorcycle like a prospector of old with his mule. Not caring one way or the other about finding precious metal ores, I'd have scrounged for enough to live on while simply enjoying life in these beautiful places. Were there prospectors like this back in the old days before trails became dirt roads, and dirt roads became highways? Before houses were built where only teepees and lodges had been erected? Before towns and cities came to the mountains?

That first extended motorcycle trip with Dave took us through Vancouver, down the coastal highway to California, back through Nevada, the Four Corners area, up through Idaho and into Montana. We visited Yellowstone National Park.

And it snowed.

It started snowing that night, and we had set up camp at the Morrison site. The toilet building was heated, so we discovered. How nice of the US Park Service to give us a little heat! Other campers discovered this blessing, and soon the men's can was crowded with both males and females. An impromptu party ensued that made an otherwise dismal night quite nice.

We met another biker, Mike, from New York. He was a lawyer and strongly left-winged on his politics. Man, did he ever fill our ears! Dave argued with him a little, but then gave up because, well, this guy Mike was a lawyer after all.

When morning came, Dave, Mike and I made a run for Old Faithful. My God we got cold. The snow was melting in the bright sunlight, but the air was still frigid and sucked the heat right out of us. By the time we reached the restaurant at Old Faithful, we were all shivering so hard we could hardly croak out an order. The waitress placed hot chocolate before us after she guessed that we might be too cold to communicate.

The hot ambrosia settled us down. We had breakfast and headed back into the wind, down to West Thumb, up toward Tower Junction and Bear Tooth Pass. The day had warmed considerably. We had no further trouble with near hypothermia.

Mike let us try out his motorcycle, a BMW, and he tried out both of ours. As long as the subject didn't turn to politics, we all got along fine. Sometimes Mike would head off into a soliloquy, Dave would redden in the face, and I wore this silly grin. Mike was good! I've not met many since who could shred myths like he could. I wonder what he is up to these days?

We split up when Dave and I headed north while Mike headed east, back to New York.

Just before crossing the South Dakota border back into Minnesota, we stopped at a little town to grab a burger. We spotted an angled parking spot to our left and swung into it, which, as we soon discovered from the local constable, is an illegal turn. The constable took us to the courthouse about a half block away where he magically turned into the local magistrate.

He fined us fifty dollars each.

Dave and I looked at each other. "Fifty dollars each?" exclaimed Dave.

"We don't have fifty dollars each," I added ruefully.

The magistrate looked a little vexed. "How about forty dollars each, then?"

We told him that no, we didn't have forty dollars each, either. The bargaining went on: Twenty? Ten?

"Oh, we can do ten dollars for the both of us. Otherwise, we won't have enough money to return home," Dave offered. The magistrate accepted our ten dollar fine.

You know, justice is a funny thing. What is funnier is justice looking out for a free lunch. Dave and I hoped the good magistrate would choke on a chicken bone. Or get a fish bone caught in his gizzard. Or eat something ripe and spend days on the can.

People can be very nice, though. While camping along the coast of Washington, Dave and I were trying to light a campfire to heat up our cans of beans. The firewood we had collected was soaked from ocean fog. Nothing was working, not even a little gasoline as an accelerant. A pair of fishermen noticed our situation and offered to help. We chatted a little about where we'd come from and where we'd been, and the fishermen decided that we were all right kids. They invited us into their camp to dine on king chinook salmon, Walla Walla sweet onions, and other fare that made our little cans of beans seem pathetic, and they were. Dave and I listened to fishing stories and other tales these two retired gentlemen shared with us as we gorged on the best tasting food we had enjoyed since leaving Minnesota.

The fishermen's camp was big and impressive. They each had pickup trucks with large campers. In addition, a cabin tent with sturdy cots had been set up. The fishermen offered us the tent and cots, and we gratefully accepted. We had slept in beds only once during the past two weeks, after eight days on the road and needing baths badly; We had taken a cheap motel where we soaked the stink off.

Next morning, we were treated to bacon and eggs before loading up the bikes and heading on out. Those fishermen were extremely nice to us, and all we had to do was eat, listen to stories, accept the hospitality, and be grateful. I don't know if there really are angels who might take human form to help out, but these guys sure fit the idea.

I contrast this with an incident that happened at a little tourist trap/restaurant in Canada. Dave and I had stopped to make some lunchmeat sandwiches, and we did this using a battered up wooden picnic table alongside the restaurant. The owner came out and shoed us away. How dare we make sandwiches near her restaurant! Bad boys, very bad boys!

We were a little shocked at this and were tempted to raise a fuss, but awe, to hell with it. We took our bread and meat to the bikes, rode a little ways to a rest stop, and made our sandwiches there.

"What a bitch, hey Dave?" I said to break the tension.

"Yeah. Ugly bitch too. Bet her old man is miserable," replied Dave. He seemed to be relaxing and the redness drained from his face.

"Whoo, do you suppose? I'd sure hate to be married to that."

"Yep."

We usually talked like that. Most men from Minnesota don't talk a whole lot, as you might have heard from the likes of Garrison Keillor. He's a writer and does a radio show on NPR. He's pretty much documented what Minnesota men are like, so I won't go into it. Let's just say that what goes on inside our heads seldom gets aired very much. Over the years, I've learned to open up a lot more, but this did not come easily. The upside is that a lot of Minnesota men are excellent listeners, and apparently, Washington fishermen appreciate this quality. So do a lot of women. In fact, I dare say I only get into trouble with women when my lips are flapping, especially after downing some brews and bumping a couple of shots.

When we returned to our little hometown, it seemed a lot smaller than when we had left. I knew right away that my urge to leave would never go away, and so, after two years of community college, I headed out to Mankato for the rest of my college education.

That motorcycle trip changed both Dave and me. It probably hangs in his memories to this day, as it does in mine, and when things seem too depressing, we can find comfort in those memories. We are at war now, and we need comforting. The news comes in from everywhere. I personally did not want this war and didn't feel especially threatened by Iraq, nor do I have anything personally against Iraq's leadership. I mean, to me it is all an abstraction. To those who have been shipped over there to fight and their families, it is all too real.

In the abstract, I see images of Saddam Hussein. I think he is a cruel dictator because that's what I've been told. I think a lot of his people have suffered under his leadership because that's what I've been told. He has tried to acquire massively lethal weapons, or so I've been told. I've been told that this war is necessary to attain peace and to make the world safer for democracy. Well, nobody is putting it across exactly like that due to the World War I slogan. Each war needs a different slogan, otherwise we'll be reminded of past failures. This one seems to be "regime change," and that is about the most lame slogan I've ever heard. "Liberate Iraq" is better, but that isn't exactly how this all got started. What started it was fear of terrorism, and from what I've seen, that motivation worked. We are at war, like it or not.

I'm feeling helpless but not like the deer caught in the headlamps. No, I saw this train coming a long way off, and I am not on the tracks, and it is broad daylight. In fact the morning sun is pouring through the French doors of my writing area right now, causing the laptop screen to wash out. Time will bring the sun higher, and time will bring this war to an end. I hope it is a very quick end, but now more doubts have been brought forth.

The Iraqi people are fighting back. What we are being told is that they fight because they are afraid that Saddam Hussein won't be bumped out of power (or killed), and that they will suffer revenge if the United States fails to remove him. In the abstract, I can believe this to be true, but in my heart, I think this is total bullshit. The Iraqi people are fighting because we have invaded their country. Saddam may be a cruel dictator, but he is their cruel dictator. It is their country. Wouldn't we fight back under similar circumstances?

Oh, I know there are huge differences between the Iraqi people and the American people. However, aren't there also similarities? Humans are pretty much the same all over. You have some jerks, you have some idiots, you have some cruel dictators, and you have some very nice folks. You have warriors with absolute courage. These warriors have families and friends. Everybody has common feelings. How would you feel if your country were to be invaded?

Some of us can imagine this, while others stubbornly insist on not imagining this. That's the nature of war. In order to be willing to do this, you have to view the enemy as being subhuman.

This morning, April 6, 2003, I awoke with a nagging fear. A vision of Baghdad exploding in a massive nuclear blast, initiated by Saddam Hussein, as US troops take the city. Baghdad, the airport, and all areas for hundreds of miles around—wiped out in a few instants. I saw in my mind's eye the video shots of the blooming mushroom cloud as hundreds of thousands of people were vaporized, hundreds of thousands more poisoned. I shuddered. Another trauma for those of us who survive. Another wave of television coverage, possibly world war.

I hope this isn't a psychic impression. I hope this does not come about. But we know Saddam Hussein is capable of such an action. What will come about in the next few days? I really hope this does not happen.

Someday, this war will be history. Many books will be written about it, I imagine. If this all works out for the better, I will be very happy. For now, I worry. I also worry about my country taking a path that may be seen in history as an extremely arrogant and naïve choice. Hope I'm wrong.

I'm wrapping this chapter up for publication. Now, the war is over, and thank God my vision turned out to be false. Nobody got nuked. Thank God.

Still, factions in Iraq continue to raise a ruckus, especially the fundamental religious folks. They want a religious government. Other factions want a democracy, and still others want Saddam back. We are told that Iraq is the size of California—that in reference to how hard it is to find those weapons of mass destruction that we wanted to stop Saddam from using on us, somehow. Maybe through the terrorist networks, maybe through a suitcase bomb attack, maybe by eating a lot of beans and blowing missiles out of their asses.

I've been proven wrong in a lot of my anxieties about this war. Good. I hope I continue to be proven wrong.

~ *14* ~
My Black Letter Fades

Since I have the time now, we are thinking about sending me back to Mankato State University (MSU) to finish my bachelor's degree in English. I don't really need a degree for working as a Unix systems administrator, which is what I was doing before the layoff, but I might want to do some graduate work after the economy turns around. The thought is to take advantage of tuition reimbursement benefits when, and if, they ever come back into my computer-related career path—or just to finish if my path continues to be a writer and an author.

Through the process of gathering information from MSU, I discovered that my records have a hold on them. The hold has a number—37—and this number has meaning: I had done something bad. Digging a bit more, it turned out that I had misrepresented myself as having a bachelor's degree in 1991.

Oh yes, I remember that. I had taken a job with a beltway bandit outfit near Washington, D.C., and upon filling out the paperwork, I was confronted with some boxes about my degree. Usually these forms just have a few checkboxes, some with a checkbox for "some college" and some without. This one wanted me to write something in there. I do remember hesitating. Should I claim a degree or not? My resume had that claim on it. Would changing my story now that I'd been hired hurt me? Ah, what a tangled web we weave, eh? There's one thing I can't stand, and that is an inconsistent liar. I've known folks who lie profusely—telling stories that just can't be true and are usually designed to raise the story teller's esteem in other people's eyes. Or at least that's the intent. I doubt if it ever really happens, unless the listener is extremely gullible. Well, come to think of it, maybe these types do impress certain other types. However that comes out in the end, I decided that if I was to be a liar, I'd better be a consistent one. But where did this lie begin? When had I transformed from a basically honest person to this disgusting liar about to pen a pile of bullpucky?

Back in the Colorado recession of the mid-1980s, I was desperate for a job. I had a fourteen-year-old to think about along with my sigoth of the time, Laurel. My job with StorageTek had disappeared as the company went into bankruptcy due to many reasons, but mostly it had overextended on several ambitious development projects. Meanwhile, the gas and oil industries in Colorado had tanked. The local job market was flooded with techies, and I was having a dickens of a time finding a new job. Not only had I moved from technical writing to mainframe systems programming, but I had gained only one year's experience in my new career direction.

A headhunter I was working with had a possible gig in Memphis, Tennessee, and suggested that I just claim a BA degree in English from Mankato instead of my standard blurb about having completed all but one quarter toward the degree and maintained a 3.4 GPA. I shrugged. Oh what the heck, go ahead, I need a job. Headhunters always like to reword resumes to direct them to the specific job opening.

The company in Memphis hired me because I had studied English, had five years of technical writing, and one year of mainframe systems programming. The company needed a good writer to document the routine work procedures of its systems programming staff. This writer needed to be able to grow into the systems programming profession, too. The headhunter thought I was the perfect candidate, but why make the college work blurb so complex? Why not just claim the BA and then, when hired, if a background check turns up the lie, I could beg forgiveness. Meanwhile, I'd have relocated from Colorado and started work. Besides, since a degree wasn't absolutely necessary for the position—it just added oomph to the resume—the chances of getting caught were very low. I thought this was making sense and went along with the scheme.

After I read this section to Lydia for her editorial comment, she told me that if she were Laurel, she would have hated me had I not lied to get that job. In her cosmology, family survival trumps personal honesty. If there's a current epidemic of resume stuffing and degree fraud, perhaps the lousy economy has a lot to do with it. Desperate people will do desperate things, as the old adage goes.

Three years later, I quit the position in Memphis to take a more challenging one in Chantilly, Virginia. As I moved through my mainframe systems programming career, the lie about having completed my degree stayed on my resume, and in retrospect, this was a horrible mistake. At the time I didn't think much of it, nor did my subsequent employers. Nobody cared if I had studied English or been a technical writer, other than I was often tasked to write reports or help write other documents. Then, fate brought me to the beltway bandit outfit and a confrontation with my lie.

The contracting outfit placed me with US Customs in Newington, Virginia. Everything was going fine for about four weeks, and then something happened that would cost me my job. Another contractor was caught in a real lollapalooza of a fib. He claimed to have an MBA from Harvard, but he had never been to college at all! That caused the beltway bandit outfit to go through all employee files to confirm education levels. I was nabbed in my stupid little fib, and even though my boss didn't want to do it, he had to fire me.

Man, did I ever fell crummy about this. Why did I lie when the job did not require a college degree of any kind? My boss asked me how much more college work I had remaining. I told him that I had about sixteen credits to go, one quarter's worth of work. He actually considered sending me back to finish, but in the end, he decided that the three months it would take was just too much time. Instead, he requested that I write a letter to the company explaining the situation. Even though I tried to spin out of the clinch hold, my letter didn't work either. I had lied and that was that. So long job.

Finding work in 1991 was also a bit difficult. The economy was just starting to pull out of the 1990 recession, but job demand had not developed as yet. Fortunately, I found a systems programming job with a regional bank and landed it without claiming a bachelor's degree. My experience was sufficient. After working the bank for two years, MCI took me on in 1993 and shipped me back to Colorado. My career zoomed along swimmingly until the layoff in November of 2001.

But now I have discovered, or actually rediscovered, this hold on my record. MSU did send me a letter about twelve years ago informing me about the hold. The only way to get it lifted was to drive to Mankato, face the judiciary board, plead my case, and take my licks. I asked Lydia if this was worth it, since attaining the degree would do little to help me find work that doesn't yet exist, and I sure don't need a degree to continue along my writing path. She thought that it would be a great idea to finish my degree anyway, because doing so would take a nasty part of my life and bury it, and then I could move ahead with graduate work if I wanted. I asked her about the expenses of gas, motels, and food. She suggested that I do research along the way for a writing project. Why sure! I could do this chapter for this book, plus look around for something else of interest along the road. Then, if something sells, I would pay her back. Lydia gave me the nod and the money to do the journey.

On my way up to Mankato, I decided to go through the Black Hills of South Dakota. There I stopped at a relatively unknown national park, Wind Cave, just south of Custer National Park. To my surprise, American bison roamed Wind Cave National Park like free-range cattle. Oh, now there's a story! I dropped by the visitor center and asked about the park and buffalo. A very helpful intern gave me quite a bit of information and history. The buffalo herd dates back to 1903, consists of about 300 head, and the excess population is sold each year on a not-for-profit basis. The genetic strain is not diluted with beef cattle, and the herd does not suffer from inbreeding, as many commercial herds do. After taking a few digital photos of a mighty bull who was grazing right alongside the road, and I think accustomed to posing for the lens, I headed over to the Crazy Horse Monument.

The Crazy Horse Monument is a massive granite mountain sculpture that makes Mount Rushmore seem very tiny in comparison. And indeed, all of the Mount Rushmore presidential sculptures could fit inside Crazy Horse's head. The full sculpture will include the head and torso of Crazy Horse, plus his horse's head and part of its body. I watched the orientation video, took a few photos, bought a video on how the blasting is done to accomplish mountain sculpturing, and hit the road again. I had two potential stories to tell.

It took me three days to reach Mankato. Coming into that river town brought back floods of memories. Yes, I had lived in that ugly green house on Warren Street. There's the old Cooper Hall where I did my last two quarters of college—Gage Hall where I started out in the A tower. The red, wavy sculpture that we students nicknamed "Lips" still kissed the sky near the library.

I visited an area right near the Blue Earth River where I lived after college while working as a motorcycle mechanic for Lakeside Cycle. Nothing had changed in twenty-eight years. The old house still stood, which amazed me because it had been in sad shape before, and it did not appear that any work had been done on it over all these years.

Downtown had become rundown. My favorite Italian restaurant, Mama Angelina's, had converted to a pawn shop. The place that offered all-you-can-eat fish night was something else, too, a fabric shop of some sort. A favorite watering hole was still there, but had its name changed? I couldn't remember what it was called before.

The town had grown quite a bit to the east side. Sprawling mall areas dominated, and there I took a motel room. I walked to a Red Lobster and ordered up a seafood feast: lobster tail, shrimp, crab, rice. Two men and a woman occupied the table next to me, and after we were done with our meals, they invited me to sit down and chat. The men were from Sweden. We had fun swapping fishing stories, and as we were leaving, the younger of the two showed me his doggy bag, which contained an untouched lobster tail. He told me that in Sweden, lobster tail is dog food. Swedes only eat the claws and roe.

I laughed, "Yah, that's a good one!"

He assured me that this is absolutely true. Well, I guess I'll have to visit Sweden then and order up some dog food.

The next day I showed up for the judicial meeting. I had a fair idea of what this was going to be like because the director of student affairs had shipped me all kinds of information, plus a copy of my incriminating and damning student file. The college had plenty of rope with which to hang me. I had even contributed some length to that rope by sending a letter to the college declaring that I had found the new job with the bank, had changed my resume to be truthful, was working on some shareware programs, didn't need no stinking degree (or words to that effect), and have a great day. So, there was no point in fighting it. I had lied.

As the meeting started, the accusation that I had lied prefaced everything else. I pleaded no contest. Yep, I had lied. The question then became, is one lie greater or lesser than another?

Well, good question. Is one lie greater or lesser than another? Had I claimed an MBA from Harvard, is that a greater lie than claiming a BA from Mankato? Actually, it isn't called Mankato State University any longer. The name had been changed to Minnesota State University as several state colleges came together in mutual agreements that, among other advantages, allow students to smoothly transfer credits among the various branches. In any case, I contended that my lie was a lesser lie. I had almost achieved my BA, but due to circumstances in 1975, I never returned to Mankato to finish.

But why? How much money would it have taken? This never came up during the meeting, but I remember perfectly what happened. I had taken a summer job with Lakeside Cycle, working just above minimum wage, setting up and fixing Harleys and Suzukis. Over the long Fourth of July weekend, I went back to my hometown of Virginia, Minnesota to celebrate with my family. Rolph, my next older brother, took me aside to ask if I was finished with college. I told him that I had one more quarter to go, and, since we had been enjoying adult beverages, the conversation became an argument. Rolph thought I was becoming a professional student. That's not so bad, but my brother was a nasty drunk. Oh boy, could he tear into you! Well, he had a point, so I thought back then. What was college doing for me? Here I was, making minimum wage in a working class job, using skills and abilities that I had not learned in college, and what the heck kind of future is that? What good was college?

One thing that needs to be understood is that none of my family goes to college. College is for the snooty upper class types on the north side of town. We lived on the south side. We were miners, mechanics, and electricians. We worked hard, played hard, and drank way too hard. We told it like it was, whether you wanted to hear about it or not. We were stubborn, strong, and bold.

Let's just say this legacy of my Northern Minnesota culture has not been an asset in my professional career with computers. Let's just say there was this meeting after a system crash in which my legacy culture rose up, and there I was, head-to-head—angry, hollering, gesturing—with the director of hardware services. Let's just say that this led to a Dale Carnegie training session for me on how to control anger, plus how to be a nice guy.

The judicial meeting started to raise my hackles as the professors in the meeting dug into my psyche. I didn't mind the students at all. They were treating me kindly, for the most part. But the professors wanted more. This caused the old working-class culture to well up in me, and a little of it came through. Not a lot, mind you, but enough to cause me to display what Lydia refers to as my Jack Nicholson face: head bowed down, eyes lowered, sometimes a fist on my knee like old uncle Bucky—a man of few but powerfully bitter words about mining company management. Uncle Bucky had a fierce way of popping his eyes out and a voice like Odin, the Norse god of war, poetry, knowledge, and wisdom. With his fist firmly planted on his knee, he would decry all the injustices of the world, especially as promoted by that gotdam management.

Anyway, returning back to 1975, I decided to stay on with the motorcycle shop through the winter to work on Arctic Cat snowmobiles. The trouble was that the winter of 1975-76 did not produce enough snow, and so I was laid off due to lack of work. My return to the working class was a miserable bust.

So, from there I did fast-food assistant management for three months—worst job I've ever had—and then moved up to Minneapolis to take a warehouse job. During the interview for that position, the manager asked me if I intended on returning to college. I had to dance furiously to convince him that I had no interest in college. That's where my legacy culture helped out. Because I got all worked up about those snooty college types, I got the job.

But that was a lie too. I didn't believe it. I had made too many friends in college, both students and faculty, to believe it. As my third year in the warehouse rolled along into the Christmas season, I happened upon a book about career development. I've mentioned this book in a previous chapter, but just as a reminder, it was Richard Bolles' *What Color Is Your Parachute*. I bought it, read it, and realized that with almost four years of college, I could do a lot better in the world than work in a warehouse.

The first thing to do was to get out of the warehouse and into a position that wasn't as comfortable. I transferred within the company to an aluminum foundry. This involved hot, dirty, loud work where I needed to wear steel-toed boots, a heavy leather apron, welder's gloves, safety glasses and goggles, ear plugs and cups, and a hardhat. The next thing to do was to save money so I could jump from one career to another. By March I was ready to jump.

My efforts with career development worked! By May, I had landed an entry-level technical writing job in computers. Did I claim a BA degree from Mankato to help gain that job? Oh, no, not at all. You see, I did not get that job on my credentials. I got it because I knew how to write, how to think for myself, how to network among professionals in the field, how to communicate and listen, and plus I had technical potential as demonstrated through my motorcycle mechanics. It also helped that the person who hired me rode a beautiful, jet black and chrome, Harley panhead chopper.

A college degree alone never gets anyone a job. A college degree is necessary for some jobs, such as college professor, lawyer, doctor and so on, but even a college professor with a doctorate degree has to be talking with the right hiring manager to land the job. I, through my own efforts and through bypassing the human resources department, was talking to exactly the right hiring manager. He had hired a tech writer, but she quit after a week because her former employer offered more money for her return. Then up I come, a guy looking for just that job and having the fire in his belly to do it. For a long time I kept a file containing both my acceptance letter and the rejection letter that had been issued weeks before by the human resources department, as a souvenir of my victory over the traditional hiring process.

The judicial meeting continued. Someone asked if I knew just how much damage I had done with my lying about having a degree. I answered:

"Oh, I know this is very important for the college and students. If everyone lied about having degrees, degrees would lose all value."

I guess that I was supposed to feel contrite and sorry for my transgression against higher education and the student body, but at the time I just could not raise a tear. I was having all I could do to keep from turning into my uncle Bucky and letting everyone have it, blasting into them with a tirade about how freaking useless degrees really are. That would have been fun but messy.

You see, it isn't all about the degree. The degree is just a symbol for something greater: education. If education does not back the degree, you might as well pay your money for a piece of worthless paper and be done with it. In fact, we call institutions that do this *diploma mills*. Is Mankato a diploma mill? Absolutely not! Why, I'm a living, walking, talking, writing, motorcycle riding, guitar playing truth that the education the student body receives and earns is highly valuable, if the student body knows what to do with that education. I've hinted at one method of promoting yourself through career development, and I highly recommend that all students study career development—and put the principles into practice. Just reading about it does nothing. You have to take action.

Now this is an issue I get worked up about. What constitutes a college education? Well, you learn how to do research, how to think for yourself, how to set goals, and how to attain these goals. Going to a college such as MSU changes a person over the course of four years. My brother Rolph could not understand that not only was I no longer working class, I could no longer return to that status—not even if I desired the return. I tried and failed! But then, I won something too. I had earned a college-level education, so my challenge had become to carry my personal metamorphosis all the way through.

As I am writing this chapter, I am also doing research on the Web regarding degree fraud. I think this would be a worthy pursuit for anyone considering a college education or currently on the quest for greater knowledge and autonomy. A college degree should indicate that the holder has risen above the level of high school, matured into a more valuable adult—both socially and economically—and has the ability to move ahead on his or her own steam. How many ways are there to earn a college education? There's really only one: You must do the work. However, what about someone who went off into life without college, or very little college, and proved to be successful? Could this person claim life experience as justifying a degree?

As it so happens, this can be done, at least at some level. A Web search on the keywords "college degree fraud" brought up several resources that mid-career adults can use to establish a degree using life experience as a basis. Is this fraud? Well, the sites I found address that issue and claim that this is not fraud, but rather a different approach to the idea of how to grant a college degree. One source argues that what a degree represents is theoretical knowledge, while life experience represents both theory and application.

Mankato sent me an article about a college professor who had lied about his degree and suffered the consequences. This guy had not completed one semester's worth of college work in his life. Yet, he had earned dominance in his field by publishing multiple books, and his reputation as an educator was top-notch. The college for which he worked decided to fire him from his six-figure income teaching job upon learning about the degree fraud. The disgraced man then went through about a year of suffering for his sin, but then arose from the ashes of his old career to do independent lecturing and teaching. He does not need a degree to freelance, only to teach in the college.

The article left me with one question: Why didn't the

professor's college simply grant him an honorary degree? I suppose there were political considerations, just as my boss in 1991 could not stick out his neck for me. That's fine. And I suppose the professor needed to take his licks, as I have been doing. There's also something social about being a college graduate, and I admit to having not a clue as to what this means. I think it comes from Medieval times, and maybe someday, after I gain my degree, someone will approach me in a darkened parking ramp, the bright light of headlamps behind him silhouetting his long robes and graduate degree hat, and in a mysteriously low, cautious voice, offer me the answer. In Medieval English, of course.

I did go through a period of self-hatred way back in 1991. To my surprise, this feeling rose up in me strongly as I drove away from Mankato after my judicial review meeting. It stuck to me as the miles rolled underneath my Jeep, the flatlands dropped behind, and beautiful Colorado came closer. As I entered my beloved adopted state, the feelings still clung. I felt as if a black letter "L" had been tattooed on my forehead. Liar! Usurper! Disgraced!

My thoughts while in these feelings revolved around the issue of whether I had done the student body wrong with my lie. Oh yes, at the emotional level, that is irrefutable. I still see the angry eyes of one student council member, the accusing stare with hateful snort. I needed to experience that. Lying is lying, even though some lies are greater and more hurtful than others. We occasionally need to lie to avoid hurting others, and the act of bestowing brutal honesty upon your loved one is usually intended to bring hurt and nothing more. However, I did not need to lie when I did. It was my choice, and for my choice, I have paid, and now repaid, penance for this mistake.

There's a moral lesson here, and I think the lesson goes

beyond the fact that lying, at least my sort of lying, brings no good and serves no purpose. The other part of the lesson is that you can't keep a good person down. Yes, the feelings are intense, and in a depressed state, might even lead to suicide. The cruelty of humans to other humans comes out, as when the professor who was caught in his lie was accused, in a grocery store, of being the disgraced poet, and this was delivered by a person who isn't even worthy of—well, I don't want to get overly crude here.

The disgraced college professor picked himself up and moved on with his life, and he will likely enjoy greater success for doing so. Perhaps, with his lack of belief in the college system for granting degrees, he really should have been an independent lecturer and educator in the first place. After all, the richest man in the world (currently) holds no degree, so if money is a measure of success, there you go. Great jazz, blues, and rock musicians tend not to hold degrees in music, as great popular writers tend not to have studied much English. We can also observe that Einstein, although trained in accounting, is remembered for his work in higher mathematics.

Does granting degrees for life accomplishments dilute the value of degrees? Actually, as it becomes more necessary to have a degree of some sort to even work in warehouses, the value—as far as differentiation goes—is diluting all on its own. As a result, some institutions have changed curriculum to focus on less traditional studies and allow at least partial credit for life experiences.

I think we need to be careful with our institutions and the credentials they bestow. We should not put too much emphasis on credentials, else we cut off our noses to spite our faces. The computer industry has traditionally recognized talent over credentials, and this is due in part to the rapid change that takes place in technology. Granted, a degree in computer science can help when entering the field, but ability is what moves one through a career in the computer industry. For this reason, many people with no college degree or even college experience of any kind have advanced through the ranks of computer technicians. Some have even successfully entered management circles and thrived.

I think also that we need to reaffirm exactly what a college education is. Is it only theory? Do we simply extend the high school model, where the rote memorization of unconnected facts to be brain-dumped during exam time becomes the goal? How many professions require this skill? Shouldn't the goals be more in line with the realities of the actual work that one will do once out of school? What about critical thinking, problem solving, research and analysis, time management, public speaking, writing, building teams, working in teams, and persuading others to your views and ideas?

I recently visited The Rocky Mountain Institute, an energy-efficient building that Amory and Hunter Lovins built in 1980 near Aspen, Colorado. Amory and Hunter are well known in ecological and business circles. Their ideas help shape national and international policies regarding, among others, energy collection and generation, pollution control, vehicular design, and urban development. Although Amory's biography lists numerous honorary degrees, it does not list a bachelor's degree. I don't know for sure, but this could indicate that he dropped out of college to promote his ideas—ideas that were radically different for the time, and as you might expect, bitterly opposed by those who held onto established ways of doing things.

What is this saying about the value of a degree? Lydia refers to it as getting the ticket punched. Is that all it is? And if so, isn't that in and of itself a lie? But then Lydia counters with the notion that some people are just plain good at what they do, but others need help. Most people, after all, are average. They need something to validate themselves, and like the Scarecrow, they need a diploma to have a brain.

The emotions in all this run deep and cold. Our established higher education institutions often reject life experience as valuable toward validation, while our business leaders often have contempt for purely theoretical intellectuals. Amory and Hunter Lovins, plus others, promote both intellectual pursuit of theory and practical application of that theory. I believe this is what higher education is all about, and what a degree must symbolize. It should not be just a ticket to get punched; it can't be only that. But the emotions are there, and the conflicts continue.

A few months back, I interviewed for a job in a group situation. Sitting next to me was a woman who expressed resentment that the technical book I had written had been commercially published. How dare I! I didn't even finish my bachelor's, and she held a master's!

What, I need a degree to convince a publisher that I can write a book that will make money? Afraid not, my book is published. But this begs the question: Where are your published works? What have you accomplished in the world? Well, I didn't say any of this. It was a job interview, and expressing yourself too honestly doesn't help the cause. However, I didn't get the job either, so I guess this wasn't a good fit.

Back in 1991, I picked myself up and moved on with my life. I stopped the lying that was doing no good and possibly causing lots of harm, not only to myself but to employers, students, and institutions. Now, twelve years later, unemployed, attempting to make a living as a freelance writer, and paying again for my transgression, I continue to move on.

Mankato sent me the results of my review. The hold has been lifted from my records to allow me to register for the summer session. Good, this is what I wanted. However, I must do some number of hours of service to the college. That's fair. And I have a few other things I must do before this whole thing is behind me for good.

So, should I finish my degree? For a while there I was about to chuck it all out the window. I don't really need the degree; I need a job—or I need to stay on this writing path, fully commit to it, and get to work! But after expending all this emotional energy, am I willing to not carry on through?

Wouldn't that be a gutless thing to do? And didn't I write above that a degree is worthless unless you have the guts to carry it on through, to become the professional whatever you are now meant to be? There's no turning back. You must move ahead.

And so I have contacted the registrar's office and asked for help in designing my coursework for the coming summer session. Lydia will sponsor me through, God bless her educated soul. My black letter "L" fades.

Epilogue

Today is June 7, 2003. I have been unemployed for nineteen months now, and over this time, I have brought two books to term. Neither have been easy to write, but the second was easier than the first. The third should be even easier, and indeed, I have it well underway.

I'm still looking for a job but without the panic, fear, and self-loathing that I once had. We were hoping to get a royalty check from the first book this month, but the sales have been flat, and the royalty advance hasn't yet been covered. However, Lydia's online work with the University of Phoenix continues to keep us in the house, and I continue to help her out in any way that I can.

The back deck is finished, the hummingbirds have returned, and this spring is bright with new green foliage and early wildflowers. What a difference from last year's early and fearful fire season! Rain has been coming regularly and the high country received more than average snowfalls, and as that melts, perhaps our reservoirs will return to normal levels.

Yet, among all this brightness and renewal, people still worry about getting laid off or they deal with unemployment. President Bush seems to have only one solution for this problem, and that is cutting taxes. He promises that a million jobs will be created through the tax cut, but we have already lost more than two million jobs since he took office. The news reported last night that the total number of unemployed citizens is now at the astounding level of nine million, or 6.1% of the workforce. More layoffs are coming, so the business analysts tell us. I'm afraid that what President Bush proposes as a solution is too little that will come too late for many people who are suffering right now, and who will soon be suffering.

The Democrats have started their runs for the White House, and they, as to be expected, are hammering Bush on domestic issues. Will better solutions be proposed and put into place? We still have months to go before election time. Will the economy recover before then? Or will we be facing two long, hot summers and possibly urban riots?

I have added my own political slant to events that happened over my months of unemployment, and I know many of you share my feelings. I've met you at a peace rally that turned ugly. I've talked with you in supermarkets, restaurants, and read your postings in online political boards. I also know many people disagree with my views of things, and that's fine. We agree to disagree. For example, I was against the war in Iraq because I feared that it would blow up in our faces. For some reason, you may have had full confidence that the war would not only be a success in the shooting part, but a success in its aftermath. I hope so, but I still have my doubts. I am not convinced that war leads to lasting solutions. I think we need to figure out better ways than war.

I hope this book helps you to understand that the feelings you may be struggling through are common. They are the normal reactions of people facing real threats on a daily basis, not the abstract fears of terrorism and war. I hope I've been able to give a few resources that might help for your situation, and I wish only the best for everyone.

Perhaps good will come out of this extended business cycle downturn. Perhaps business and government will come out being more clean, more efficient, and better planned to sustain moderate levels of growth and high levels of employment for many years to come. I can't help but feel that we have been betrayed by WorldCom, Enron, Global Crossing, and all the other corporations who have been caught cooking their books.

And even with all the problems that have come with unemployment, we have also endured through the terrorist attack of 9/11, the resulting war in Afghanistan, and the recent war in Iraq. People have gone a little crazy on all sides of the political map, and this has all happened within the past year and a half or so. How much more can happen over the coming year? By Election Day?

Lydia and I have been very lucky through all this. We are lucky in that the love we share is made of the true stuff. We are lucky that we've been able to keep enough money coming in to live, but not enough to plan much for the future. I know other people have not been so lucky. I know, from experience, that unemployment and the insecurity that breeds, along with the intense emotions involved, can lead to harsh words being said and foolish actions being done that can never be forgiven.

In its worst expression, unemployment can lead to riots in the streets, the forming of radical political groups, the oppression of innocent citizens, and solutions that ultimately prove to be huge mistakes. Our history shows how this can happen, and I sure don't want to even come close to repeating that history. We don't need another round of unionization, union busting, American communism, or McCarthyism. Do we really want another New Deal? Aren't we smarter than this, more creative?

We were so hopeful through the 1990s. We thought our economy had reached a new level of stability that defied the business cycle. People started families, bought houses, settled down, and worked with gusto and joy. Nothing seemed impossible as we built and improved and made things happen.

Will we ever regain that hopefulness?

I want to end this book with a simple plea to those who control our government and economy. I want to ask them to please try to find better ways of doing things so that families and singles aren't put through long terms of unemployment that force people into bankruptcy, break up families, and throw good people out on the street with no income, no health insurance, great fear and self-doubt, and little hope for the future. This is not what America is supposed to be about.

We are supposed to be better than this.

Printed in the United States
1487200001B/19-69